西安交通大学"十四五"规划教材
西安交通大学少年班规划教材·英语

BRIDGE TO COLLEGE

U0747864

阅读与写作(1)

READING AND WRITING FOR ACADEMIC STUDY

牛莉◎总主编
成旻 龚颖◎本册主编
成旻 高菲 龚颖 牛莉◎编者

西安交通大学出版社
XI'AN JIAOTONG UNIVERSITY PRESS

图书在版编目(CIP)数据

阅读与写作. 1 / 牛莉总主编；成旻，龚颖本册主
编. — 西安：西安交通大学出版社，2020.9(2025.8重印)
西安交通大学少年班规划教材. 英语
ISBN 978 - 7 - 5605 - 9626 - 6

Ⅰ. ①阅… Ⅱ. ①牛… ②成… ③龚… Ⅲ. ①英语－
阅读教学－高等学校－教材 ②英语－写作－高等学校－教材
Ⅳ. ①H319.39

中国版本图书馆 CIP 数据核字(2020)第 131658 号

书　　　名	阅读与写作(1)
总 主 编	牛　莉
本册主编	成　旻　龚　颖
责任编辑	李　蕊

出版发行	西安交通大学出版社
	(西安市兴庆南路 1 号　邮政编码 710048)
网　　址	http://www.xjtupress.com
电　　话	(029)82668357　82667874(市场营销中心)
	(029)82668315(总编办)
传　　真	(029)82668280
印　　刷	西安五星印刷有限公司

开　　本	720mm×1000mm　1/16	印张　10.125	字数　200 千字
版次印次	2020 年 9 月第 1 版　2025 年 8 月第 4 次印刷
书　　号	ISBN 978 - 7 - 5605 - 9626 - 6
定　　价	38.00 元

如发现印装质量问题，请与本社市场营销中心联系。
订购热线：(029)82665248　(029)82667874
投稿热线：(029)82668531　(029)82665371
读者信箱：xjtu_rw@163.com

总序

Foreword

　　1985 年对西安交通大学来说是一个值得铭记的年份。这一年,教育部正式批准学校开办少年班,学校积极响应邓小平同志的指示:"在人才的问题上,要特别强调一下,必须打破常规去发现、选拔和培养杰出的人才。"转眼间,少年班已走过了三十五年的办学历程,在破解"如何发现智力超常少年并因材施教"这一极具挑战性的难题上,西安交通大学先后有五位校长,他们艰难探索,矢志不渝,构建了一套适合中国国情且自主创新的少年班人才选拔和培养体系,培养了一批又一批少年英才。目前,少年班从初中应届毕业生中选拔招生,实行"预科—本科—硕士"八年制贯通培养模式,其中,预科一年级在指定的四所优秀预科中学学习,预科二年级在大学学习,各为期一年。

　　基础教育与高等教育的有机衔接一直是少年班探索和研究的重点,而教材作为知识衔接的重要载体,成为影响少年班教育质量的关键因素。为此,钱学森学院于 2010 年 10 月成立少年班教材编写小组,正式启动教材编写研究工作。全国首套少年班系列教材出版于 2014 年 12 月。来自大学及高中的近 60 名专家和一线教师参与其中,谨遵"因材施教,发掘潜能,注重创新,超常教育,培养英才"的指导思想,通过多次研讨、仔细斟酌、反复修订和严格审核,耗时四年有余,最终编写并出版了全国首套将"预科—本科"有机衔接的教材。这套教材包含六门课程,共 22 册,总计 2550 学时,828 万字。这套教材自出版至今,使用效果良好。

　　2018 年,经过大量调研,钱学森学院制定了新版少年班培养方案,在新版培养方案的基础上规划修订数学、物理、化学、英语等课程的教材,并于 2020 年启动少年班"十四五"规划教材的编写出版工作。此版教材将力求实现"预科—本科"课程的无缝衔接,从知识体系、内容结构、案例设计、习题配套等方面对教材内涵和风格进行重新编撰和优化,同时注重拔尖学生的发展需求,体现新版少年班培养方案中"以兴趣为导向"的教育教学改革思想。

　　愿此版教材可让更多关注少年班的有识之士受益。同时,我们也希望借此机会,号召大家集思广益,群策群力,共同为推动少年英才培养进程做出努力。

　　是为序。

杨　森

2020 年 8 月 10 日

从 2012 年开始接手少年班的教学工作,我们的教学团队一直在探索适合少年班的英语教学模式,包括课程设置、教学内容、教学方法与手段、评价方式及教材等。2018 年我校钱学森学院重新制定了少年班培养方案,我们团队也借此机会对我们的教学模式重新进行了梳理,决定开设两门英语课程:"阅读与写作(Reading and Writing for Academic Study)"和"交流与表达(Communication for Academic Study)"。因此,为这两门课程而编写的两套同名教材应运而生。同时,基于少年班英语课程培养方案的总目标,即"帮助学生完成从通用英语(English for General Purpose,EGP)到学术英语(English for Academic Study,EAS)的过渡,为学生进入大学学习做好语言能力的准备",我们又将这两套教材的编写内容进行了有机结合,构成了"通往大学"系列(*Bridge to College*)。

本系列教材有三个特色:

一、教材编写突出体现"以学习为中心"和以"成果为导向"的教学理念,如下图所示:

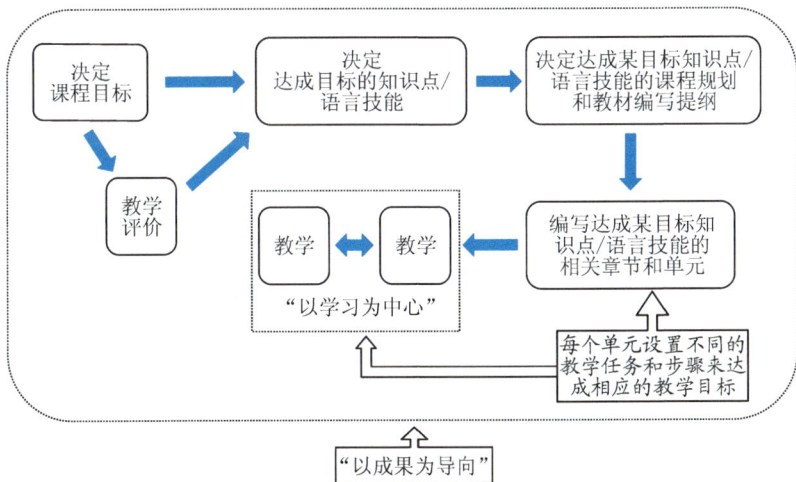

二、教材章节编排侧重构建英语语言知识和技能体系。与一般英语教材中以话题为章节(theme-based)的编写原则不同,本教材采用以功能为章节(function-based,即突出对语言知识点和技能的培养)的编写原则。因为,以话题为章节的编写理念侧重扩充相关话题的词汇量或表达,忽视了语言知识点或

语言技能之间的相关性,缺乏系统性,会导致学生在学习之后只能想起某些课文的内容;而本教材以功能为章节进行编写,其目的在于帮助学生获得相关知识点或技能,同时也帮助学生构建出完整的英语语言知识和技能体系。

三、教材内容融入教学设计。本教材中的各个章节,不仅是学生应掌握的相关知识点,同时也是教师在教学中的具体目标。本教材的章节编排突破了传统英语教材"课文+练习"的模式,变为"通过设置不同的教学任务和步骤来达成相应的教学目标"的模式。这样的编写模式,既包含了学生学习的过程,也体现了教师教学的过程,实现了"以学习为中心",即"教师为主导,学生为主体"的教学理念。

基于上述编写特点,本系列教材也适用于高中生和本科生自主学习。

最后,特别感谢各位编写老师牺牲难得的假期投入教材编写工作!特别感谢交大附中的刘晏辰老师对预科一年级教材讲义初稿的试用和及时的意见反馈!特别感谢少年班 2017 级、2018 级的同学们对教材讲义试用和新教学模式探索的积极配合和肯定!特别感谢西安交通大学钱学森学院和外国语学院给予我们团队的各种支持!特别感谢我们教学团队(包括各中学和大学的所有老师)的辛勤付出!

牛 莉

2020 年暑假

目 录
Table of Contents ▶

SECTION

1

Writing a Good Sentence

Module 1   Basic Elements in a Sentence

When finishing the learning of this module,

Goal 1   I will know basic elements in a sentence.

Goal 2   I will know different forms of each basic element.

Goal 3   I will know basic sentence patterns.

Section 1   Writing a Good Sentence

TASK ONE

Analyzing Basic Elements in a Sentence

ACTIVITY ▶

Analyzing the sentences to find out basic elements in sentences

Step 1

Work individually and divide each of the following sentences into several parts, according to the function of each part in the sentence.

1. The little boy laughed happily.
2. The students are visiting a museum.
3. Working 10 hours a day makes the workers very tired.
4. The only home for man to live on is the earth.
5. Mr. Johnson taught us German last year.
6. I got the impression that you were unhappy.

7. Here comes our headmaster.

8. It is said that all living things need light and heat from the sun to live.

9. He finally realized that the problem was extremely serious.

10. Mr. Wang，my child's teacher，will be visiting us this Tuesday.

Step 2

Work in groups of 3-4 members and discuss the basic parts in the sentences given in Step 1.

1. What are the two most common basic elements in every sentence?

2. What other basic elements are needed to make every sentence complete?

3. What is the usual order of these basic elements? Is there any unusual order used?

Step 3

Work in your group and summarize.

Basic elements needed to make complete sentences：

- _____

- _____

- _____

- _____

- _____

- _____

TASK TWO

Identifying Forms of Basic Elements

ACTIVITY ▶

Discussing and finding out different forms of the basic elements

Step 1

Work in pairs. Read the 10 sentences given in Step 1, TASK ONE, and find out the forms of the basic elements in each sentence.

Subject	Predicate	Object	Predicative	Appositive

1. _____ verb _____

2. _____ noun _____

3. _____

4. _____ noun _____

5. _____

6. _____ clause _____

7. _____

8. _____

9. __ pronoun _____

10. _____

┌ ─ ─ ─ ─ ─ ┐
│ **Step 2** │
└ ─ ─ ─ ─ ─ ┘

Work in pairs and find out more forms of the basic elements in the following sentences.

1. He can't have finished reading the 800-page-long novel.

   _____

2. The kings of ancient Egypt had strong tombs built for themselves.

   _____

3. What he said does not matter.

   _____

4. There lived an old fisherman in the village.

   _____

5. The books are on the desk.

   _____

6. The trouble is that they are short of money.

   _____

7. He ate what was left over.

   _____

8. He showed me how to run the machine.

   _____

9. We Chinese people always consider it our duty to take care of the old.

   _____

10. Only when it began to rain did she find that her umbrella was missing.

    _____

11. My dream is to become a doctor, and to prevent people from illnesses.

    _____

12. Some subjects, such as maths and physics, are very difficult to learn.

_____

Step 3

Discuss in groups of 3-4 members and summarize all the possible forms for each kind of basic elements.

Forms of Subject: _____

Forms of Predicate: _____

Forms of Object: _____

Forms of Predicative: _____

Forms of Appositive: _____

Forms of Complement: _____

TASK THREE

Understanding Basic Sentence Patterns

ACTIVITY ▶

Finding out basic sentence patterns

Step 1

Work in pairs and analyze the 10 sentences given in Step 1, TASK ONE as required.

1. Find out the sentence patterns (the order of basic elements) used in each sentence.

　(1) _____

　(2) _____

(3) _____

(4) _____

(5) _____

(6) _____

(7) _____

(8) _____

(9) _____

(10) _____

Step 2

Work in groups of 3-4 members. Analyze the 12 sentences given in Step 2, TASK TWO as required.

Find out the sentence patterns (the order of basic elements) used in each sentence.

(1) _____

(2) _____

(3) _____

(4) _____

(5) _____

(6) _____

(7) _____

(8) _____

(9) _____

(10) _____

(11) _____

(12) _____

Step 3

Discuss in your group about the kinds of basic sentence patterns that are commonly used.

1. Find out the two most general kinds of sentence patterns, with the basic elements being in opposite orders.

   Pattern Ⅰ : _____

   Pattern Ⅱ : _____

2. Find out more sentence patterns for each of the two general sentence patterns.

   Pattern Ⅰ :

   (1) _____

   (2) _____

   (3) _____

   (4) _____

   (5) _____

   Pattern Ⅱ :

   (1) _____

   (2) _____

   (3) _____

   (4) _____

   (5) _____

ASSIGNMENTS

Learn grammar about dependent clauses by yourself, and summarize:

1. Different types of dependent clauses;
2. The Basic structures of each kind of dependent clauses;
3. The Uses of each kind of dependent clauses.

Module 2   Different Elements and Structures in Sentences

When finishing the learning of this module,

Goal 1   I will be able to identify different elements in a sentence.

Goal 2   I will understand ellipsis and substitution in a sentence.

Goal 3   I will understand structures of different types of sentences.

Goal 4   I will get to know independent clause and different dependent clauses.

Section 1   Writing a Good Sentence

TASK ONE

Identifying Different Elements in a Sentence

ACTIVITY ▶

Learning to identify different types of elements in a sentence

Step 1

Work individually and underline the basic elements in the following sentences. You may refer to the information box on the next page.

Example: This is my sister Lily. (Subject ＋ Link Verb ＋ Predictive ＋ Appositive)

1. We all like this book.
2. Keeping working hard is difficult.
3. To go to a good university is her first goal.
4. My parents tell me that they enjoy listening to classical music.

5. The boy, usually a silent student, argued with his classmates in class.
6. His boss sent him the message that he would be promoted.
7. His boss sent him the message that made him very happy.

Basic Elements in Sentences
- Subject
- Predicate (*verb* or *link verb*)
- Object
- Predicative
- Appositive

Step 2

Work in pairs and find out which kind of element each underlined part belongs to, and what role each kind of element plays in the sentence.

1. This is one of her favorite cities.
2. The number of people who move to this town is still unknown.
3. —Your team played very well in last season, and they will do well this year.
   —Yes, I hope so.
4. What do you think I should do to make her change her mind?
5. We have a lot of homework to do.
6. I want to go travelling this summer, which I have been planning for many weeks.
7. When not taking training, the athlete would like to listen to music to get relaxed.
8. The expert has made another discovery, which I think is of great scientific value.
9. The exhibition is more impressive than expected.
10. If they win this game, they will break the record.
11. While her sister is playing computer games, she is helping her mother with the housework.
12. As she grew older, she realized the importance of being with family.

Summarize the type of element and the role of each underlined part in these sentences.

No.	Type of Element	Role of the Element
1	Attributive	to modify _____
2	Adverbial	to modify _____
3	Complement	to make the information or idea complete
4	Parenthesis	to indicate interruption and to add information

Step 3

Identify and distinguish attributives from adverbials in the sentences below.

1. Do you know the girl sitting beside the window?
2. Generally speaking, they are still able to choose the subjects by themselves.
3. During the summer holiday, I have a lot of homework to do.
4. Are there anything new recently?
5. The woman downstairs got home very late last night.
6. Having finished her work, she agreed to get a couple of drinks with her friends.
7. To get admitted into this club, the dancer keeps practicing for three months.
8. I like novels written by Lu Xun.
9. Located in the south of the country, the city has a high rainfall.

Step 4

Work in groups of 3-4 members, read the examples given below and summarize the locations and the forms of parenthesis in sentences.

Examples:

1. Generally speaking, the project cannot be finished in time.
2. You can, if you please, join us in the next round.
3. Strange, there is nobody in the classroom.
4. Whom do you think I should interview first?
5. On the contrary, we should strengthen our ties with them.
6. All in all, her condition is greatly improved.
7. Painted white, the house looks beautiful.

8. To be frank, I don't quite agree with you.

9. This man, as you know, is good for nothing.

10. Luckily for you, I happen to have the key.

Step 5

Put the parenthesis in brackets into these sentences and make new sentences.

1. He must be an honest person. (judged from what he says and does)

   _____

2. One day, the emperor agreed to meet the messenger. (it is said)

   _____

3. What can I do to make him happy again? (do you believe)

   _____

TASK TWO

Understanding Ellipsis and Substitution

ACTIVITY ▶

Understanding ellipsis and substitution in sentences

Step 1

Work in groups of 3-4 members, read the examples and summarize the types and uses of omitted or substituted elements in the following sentences.

Examples:

1. Sounds like a good idea.

2. They learn French and we, English.

3. I don't like the way he talks.

4. When reading, he could not concentrate because of the noise.

5. We will do what we can to help you.

6. —Would you like to take a walk with me?

—I'd love to.

7. They don't plan to go travelling during this holiday, neither <u>do</u> I.

8. —This is not the entrance to this building. —I suppose <u>not</u>.

9. —I think we will win the final game. —We all believe <u>so</u>.

10. We trust Smith. I wish we can say <u>the same</u> of his partner.

Your answers:

• Types of omitted elements:

• Uses of omitted elements:

(a) To make the sentence _____

(b) To avoid _____

---

1. Ellipsis/Omission

Ellipsis/Omission happens when we <u>leave out</u> (in other words, when we don't use) items which we would normally expect to use in a sentence if we followed the grammatical rules. The following examples show uses of ellipsis. The items left out are in brackets [ ]:

• *I am absolutely sure [that] I have met her somewhere before.*

• *She sang and [she] played the violin at the same time.*

• *He wrote to [everyone he could think of who might help] and [he] phoned everyone he could think of who might help.*

2. Substitution

In English grammar, substitution is the <u>replacement</u> of a word or a phrase with a "filler" word (such as *one*, *so*, or *do*) to avoid repetition.

Step 2

Carefully read the examples given in the information box above, and cross out the parts that can be omitted or replaced in the following sentences, and rewrite the sentences by using ellipsis or substitution.

1. My sister is singing and my sister is dancing.

_____

2. My father is thin and my mother is fat.

3. Peter finished three tasks, but Mary did two tasks.

4. You can do what you want to do.

5. He can swim faster than I can swim.

6. He ate more food than I ate.

7. You see only part of the problem, but you do not see the whole problem.

8. They can speak Chinese, and Kate can speak Chinese, too.

Step 3

Read the poem below and work out what the word "one" refers to in lines 2 and 4.

Purple Cow

1895

I never saw a Purple Cow,

I never hope to see one;

But I can tell you, anyhow,

I'd rather see than be one.

Your answer:

In lines 2 and 4, the word "one" is a substitute term for _____.

Step 4

Make sentences with words or expressions required below, by using parenthesis and/or substitution.

1. so do (does) ... / neither do (does) ...

_____

2. ... think (hope/believe/appear/expect) so (not) ...

_____

3. when (if) ... , one ...

_____

4. do (to do) ... , so ...

_____

TASK THREE
Understanding Different Sentence Structures

ACTIVITY ▶

Understanding and identifying different sentence structures

Step 1

Review the five sentence patterns by making five sentences.

1. Subject + Predicate (*vi.*)

_____

2. Subject ＋ Predicate (*vt.*) ＋ Object

_____

3. Subject ＋ Predicate (*vt.*) ＋ Indirect object ＋ Direct object

_____

4. Subject ＋ Predicate (*vt.*) ＋ Object ＋ Complement

_____

5. Subject ＋ Predicate (Link *v.* ＋ Predicative)

_____

Independent Clause

An independent clause is a group of words which constitute at least a subject and a predicate. Unlike a dependent clause, an independent clause is grammatically complete—that is, **it can stand alone as a sentence** and express a complete thought.

Step 2

Work in pairs and identify the differences in the following sentences in terms of the sentence structures.

1. The time the final decision to be made is uncertain.
2. You have to write as many songs as possible, you know, if you want to be successful.
3. Chinese dishes are delicious, but some of them are extremely calorie-rich.
4. He wants to attend the party that is to be held on Sunday, but he is not sure whether he can finish his work in time.
5. Have you heard the news that Mr. Wang will take the place of our manager to attend the meeting?
6. If you think you can do it, just go and do it, but do not complain later that I didn't warn you.

Step 3

Work in pairs and answer the following questions.

1. What is the biggest difference between the sentences you made in Step 1 and the sentences given in Step 2?

2. All sentences you made in Step 1 are independent clauses, and all sentences given in Step 2 have dependent clauses included. What are the differences between independent clauses and dependent clauses?

3. What kinds of dependent clauses have you found in sentences given in Step 2?

Dependent Clause

A dependent clause is a clause that provides an independent clause with additional information, but which **CANNOT stand alone as a sentence.** Dependent clauses either modify the independent clause of a sentence or serve as a component in a complete sentence.

Step 4

Work in pairs and summarize the four types of sentence structures, based on your work done in Step 1 to Step 3.

Type of Sentence	Structure of the Sentence
Simple Sentence	
Compound Sentence	
Complex Sentence	
Compound-Complex Sentence	

TASK FOUR

Understanding Dependent Clauses in Sentences

ACTIVITY ▶

Indentifying and understanding dependent clauses in sentences

Step 1

Identify different types of dependent clauses in the following sentences.

1. Are you interested in the activity that we help raise money for the people losing homes in the earthquake?
2. What he says is quite different from what he does.
3. It sounds as if someone is knocking at the door.
4. What would you do if your parents refuse to support you?
5. I think that I have reached the point where I should make decisions.
6. Do you know the reason why he gives up this opportunity?
7. That the couple is not satisfied with the house design is unpredictable.

Step 2

Work in pairs and summarize the types and roles of dependent clauses.

Types of Dependent Clauses		Roles of Dependent Clauses in Sentences
1.		attributive, modifying nouns
2. Adverbial Clause		
3. Noun Clause		
	Predicative Clause	
	Appositive Clause	

Step 3

Discuss in groups of 3-4 members. Highlight the relative pronouns and relative adverbs in attributive clauses in the following sentences, and analyze the grammatical roles of these relative pronouns or relative adverbs in the attributive clauses.

1. Mozi was another teacher who was very influential.
2. The girl whom I saw is called Mary.
3. There his parents bought a candy store which they ran for the next 40 or so years.
4. Is she the girl that sells newspaper?
5. Workers built shelters for survivors whose homes had been destroyed.
6. Ancient China was a place where states were often at war with each other.
7. We live in an age when more information is available with greater ease than ever before.
8. This is the reason why he was late for school.
9. He finished college at fifteen, which I found hard to believe.
10. As I have pointed out, it is important to include vegetables in our diet.

Step 4

Make eight sentences with an attributive clause included in each sentence, by using the relative pronouns or relative adverbs used in the sentences given in Step 3.

1. _____

2. _____

3. _____

4. _____

5. _____

6. _____

7. _____

8. _____

Step 5

Work in groups of 3-4 members to check and improve the sentences you have made in Step 4.

Step 6

Discuss in your group to find out different roles of the noun clauses in the following sentences.

1. That everything in the world changes is often a theme in poetry.
2. The problem is who will take charge of this shop.
3. I asked her whether she had looked at a map yet.
4. I've got a feeling that one day he will be famous.

Step 7

Discuss in your group to understand the meanings of the adverbial clauses in the following sentences, and make sentences with the conjunctions used in these adverbial clauses.

1. It was some time before I realized the truth.
2. You're not going out until you've finished this.
3. He hasn't got any hobbies—unless you call watching TV a hobby.
4. I want to see him the moment he arrives.
5. Just because I don't complain, people think I'm satisfied.
6. It was still so painful so I went to see a doctor.
7. I was about to take a shower when the phone rang.
8. You can go swimming while I'm having lunch.
9. As she grew older she gained by confidence.
10. We've lived here since 2008.

ASSIGNMENTS

1. **Learn grammar about non-finite verbs, and summarize:**
   a. Different types of non-finite verbs;
   b. The Basic structure of each kind of non-finite verbs;
   c. The Use of each kind of non-finite verbs;
   d. The Logical subject of different types of non-finite verbs.

2. **Preview TASK ONE in Module 3 about subject-verb agreement.**

Module 3   Identifying Modifiers in Sentences

When finishing the learning of this module,

Goal 1   I will be able to identify subject-verb disagreement in writing.

Goal 2   I will be able to identify different forms of attributives and adverbials.

Goal 3   I will understand the uses of non-finite verbs.

Section 1   Writing a Good Sentence

TASK ONE

Identifying Subject-Verb Disagreement

ACTIVITY ▶

Indentifying subject-verb disagreement in writing

Step 1

Work in groups of 3-4 members and find out mistakes in the following sentences.

1. Confucius were a great philosopher in ancient China.
2. He take exercise every day to keep fit.
3. They studies very hard in order to realize their dream.
4. These book are delivered to students who has no access to public library.
5. A number of actor will star in the movie.
6. The Great Wall were one of the most famous tourist attraction in China.

7. A quantity of ancient buildings in this city were designed by unknown architects.

8. A great deal of money have been earned though the company face fierce competition in Chinese market.

9. Quantities of time has been spent but they don't make any progress.

10. The writer and teacher are very popular among students.

11. Neither of my parents like to clean the house.

12. Ten years are a long time to finish a novel.

13. The rest of the students is playing football on the playground.

14. The number of the actors nominated for the best actor haven't been decided.

15. Not only I but also my sister want to go swimming in the lake.

Step 2

Discuss in the same group and summarize the general kinds of mistakes in the sentences given in Step 1, and then classify the mistakes into different types.

1. Subject-verb disagreement is the kind of mistake in which _____

_____

    a. Disagreement in _____

    b. Disagreement in _____

Step 3

Work individually and correct the mistakes in the following paragraph.

Crime have its own cycles, a magazine reports some years before. Police records that is studied for five years from over 2400 cities and towns shows a surprised link between changes in the season and crime patterns. The pattern of crime have varied very little over a long period of years. Murder reached its high during July and August, as does rape and other violent attacks. Murder, however, was more than seasonal: it is a weekend crime. It is also a high time crime: 62 percent of murders is committed between 6 p.m. and 6 a.m.

TASK TWO

Identifying Modifiers in Simple Sentences

ACTIVITY ▶

Analyzing different forms of modifiers in simple sentences

Step 1

Work in pairs. Underline attributives or adverbials in the sentences below.

1. There is something strange on the floor.
2. He is the most famous violinist alive.
3. The weather in Beijing is colder than that in Hainan.
4. He lost his way in the town full of cars.
5. Do you know the language spoken in that country?
6. I have a lot of homework to do today.
7. The sleeping girl is Anna.
8. He will contact the participants by letter.
9. She comes here specially to see the old friend.
10. Given more time, I'm sure I will finish the task in time.

Step 2

Two pairs work together. Check your work in Step 1, summarize the different forms of attributives and adverbials in the sentences above, and identify different types of adverbials.

1. Forms of Attributives: _____

2. Forms of Adverbials: _____

3. Types of Adverbials: _____

Step 3

Add attributives or adverbials, in proper forms, to complete the following sentences.

1. _____, there were many clean rivers in this village.

2. _____, he didn't remember where the document was.

3. _____, he decided to consider these choices again.

4. _____, they will go out for a walk.

5. The government will adopt the new policy, _____.

6. The band will not tour in those cities _____.

7. The policemen are investigating the case _____.

8. The company will stop producing this kind of cars _____.

9. This is the best restaurant _____.

10. The reason _____ is still a secret.

TASK THREE

Understanding Uses of Different Non-finite Verbs

ACTIVITY ▶

Understanding uses of different non-finite verbs

Step 1

Discuss in groups of 3-4 members. Underline non-finite verbs in the following sentences, and identify the type and the element of each non-finite verb in each sentence.

1. I stand outside waiting for Mrs. Carson.

2. Sometimes climbing mountain is very challenging.

3. Having finished my work, I had a short rest.

4. Our work is to help the persons in need.

5. The school basketball team is said to have accepted a good training.

6. He often studies in the reading room.

7. Having been criticized by his teacher, the student was in a bad mood.

8. The work to be finished tomorrow is not important.

9. The task is reported to have been completed by the engineers.

10. I like dishes cooked by my parents.

Step 2

Discuss the following questions in your group again.

1. How do you understand "non-finite verbs"? When do we use non-finite verbs in sentences?

2. What are the logical subjects of different non-finite verbs?

3. What are the relations among the predicates, the non-finite verbs and their logical subjects in sentences given in Step 1?

4. Group the 10 sentences in Step 1, according to the use of infinitive, gerund and participle.

5. Analyze the basic structures and uses of different non-finite verbs and complete the table below.

Non-finite Verbs	Structure	Uses
Infinitive		
Gerund		
Participle		

Step 3

Work in pairs. Make up sentences with infinitives, gerunds or participles used properly in the sentences. The number of sentences depends on your understanding of non-finite verbs and your creativity. Your work will be checked in the next class.

ASSIGNMENTS

Review grammar about tenses, passive voice and irregular verbs:

1. Different types of tenses;
2. The past tense and the past participle of irregular verbs (Keep them in mind!);
3. The uses of passive voice:
   a. Group the 10 sentences given in Step 1, TASK THREE, according to the uses of passive voice and active voice.
   b. Answer the question: When should we use passive voice and active voice?

Module 4　Writing Compound Sentences Correctly

When finishing the learning of this module,

Goal 1　I will be able to write compound sentences correctly.

Goal 2　I will learn how to avoid comma splice and sentence fragments.

Goal 3　I will be able to use passive voice properly.

Section 1　Writing a Good Sentence

TASK ONE

Writing Compound Sentences

ACTIVITY ▶

Learning to write compound sentences correctly

Step 1

Read the examples below. Work individually, find compound sentences in the following sentences and summarize the structures of compound sentences.

Examples

Compound Sentence

- He is afraid of losing again, yet he never gives up.
- "It was the best of times, it was the worst of times." —Charles Dickens
- The restaurant is very crowded; we have to have our lunch taken away.

Complex Sentence
- She didn't know whether they will come back or not.

Compound-Complex Sentence
- I think I will accept this offer, as I don't have any other better choices.

1. The student did not cheat on the test, for it was not the correct thing to do.

2. The hotel will be redecorated because the typhoon has done damage to the roof of the hotel.

3. The doctor insisted that the old woman should come back next week for another physical examination, but she declined.

4. I will buy the red motorbike, or I will lease the black one.

5. I'm losing weight, but I really want to have dessert.

6. It was cold at that night, and we didn't have any money.

7. France is my favorite country; I plan to spend three weeks there next year.

8. "I have often wanted to drown my troubles, but I can't get my wife to go swimming." —Jimmy Carter

9. He didn't want to see the doctor, yet he went anyway.

10. He ran out of money, so he had to stop spending so much on collecting stamps.

11. The authorities were not sympathetic to the students' demands, neither would they tolerate any disruption.

12. I do every single bit of house work, while my husband just does the dishes now and then.

Step 2

Work in pairs. Make a list of all the conjunctions used in the compound sentences given in Step 1 and the meanings of these conjunctions.

Step 3

Find out the use of punctuation in the compound sentences in Step 1, and summarize proper use of punctuation in compound sentences.

- Punctuation used: _____

- Proper ways to use:

  (1)　_____

  (2)　_____

  (3)　_____

Step 4

Make compound sentences with every conjunctions used in the compound sentences in Step 1.

TASK TWO

Avoiding Comma Splice in Writing

ACTIVITY ▶

Understanding the uses of comma in sentence writing

Step 1

Discuss in groups of 3-4 members, find out wrong uses of punctuation in the following sentences, and make proper correction where necessary.

1. I waited for my friend to answer my E-mail, he didn't reply to me at all.
2. His major in university hasn't been decided; but he's interested in journalism.
3. Playing piano and singing songs are his hobbies. However, he never wants to make a living of them.
4. He hasn't practiced playing table tennis for a long time, so he gained much weight.
5. It's reported to be sunny tomorrow, but you'd better bring an umbrella.
6. The author will stop writing this popular novel; his readers are very upset

about this news.

7. His parents are busy with work all the time so he has learnt to take good care of himself from an early age.

8. It's a good day to plant trees, they begin to seek tools for planting trees without hesitation.

☺**Friendly reminder**

Compare the right compound sentences and the wrong compound sentences in Step 1 and summarize the uses of comma, linking words and semicolon in compound sentences.

Step 2

Work in pairs. Improve the wrong sentences in Step 1 with proper uses of comma, linking words and semicolon, and rewrite the sentences.

TASK THREE
Avoiding Sentence Fragments in Writing

ACTIVITY ▶

Identifying and correcting sentence fragments

Step 1

The underlined parts in the following sentences are sentence fragments. Work in groups of 3-4 members and find out the problem in each fragment.

1. Purdue offers many majors in engineering. Such as electrical, chemical, and industrial engineering.

2. Coach Dietz exemplified this behavior by walking off the field in the middle of

a game. Leaving her team at a time when we needed her.

3. I need to find a new roommate. Because the one I have now isn't working out too well.

4. The current city policy on housing is incomplete as it stands. Which is why we believe the proposed amendments should be passed.

5. A story with deep thoughts and emotions.

6. Toys of all kinds thrown everywhere.

7. A record of accomplishment beginning when you were first hired.

8. With the ultimate effect of all advertising is to sell the product.

9. By paying too much attention to polls can make a political leader unwilling to propose innovative policies.

10. For doing freelance work for a competitor got Phil fired.

Step 2

Work individually and improve the sentences in Step 1.

1. _____

2. _____

3. _____

4. _____

5. _____

6. _____

7. _____

8. _____

9. _____

10. _____

Step 3

Check your work with your classmates.

TASK FOUR

Understanding the Uses of Passive Voice

ACTIVITY ▶

Learning to use passive voice properly in writing

Step 1

Work individually and do the match exercise below to summarize when passive voice should be used.

1. The cave paintings of Lascaux were made in the Upper Old Stone Age.	A. The actor is unknown.
2. Mistakes were made.	B. You want to emphasize the person or thing acted on. For example, it may be your main topic.
3. An experimental solar power plant will be built in the Australian desert.	C. The actor is irrelevant.
4. Rules are made to be broken.	D. You are talking about a general truth.
5. The sodium hydroxide was dissolved in water. This solution was then titrated with hydrochloric acid.	E. You want to be vague about who is responsible.
6. Insulin was first discovered in 1921 by researchers at the University of Toronto. It is still the only treatment available for diabetes.	F. You are writing in a scientific genre that traditionally relies on passive voice. Passive voice is often preferred in lab reports and scientific research papers, most notably in the Materials and Methods section.

Step 2

Work individually and make five sentences with passive voice used in the different ways listed in Step 1.

1. _____

2. _____

3. _____

4. _____

5. _____

Step 3

Share your sentences with your classmates and discuss the uses of passive voice in each sentence.

ASSIGNMENTS

Learn grammar about attributive clauses and appositive clauses:

1. Different types and uses of attributive clauses;
2. Uses of appositive clauses;
3. Differences between attributive clauses and appositive clauses.

Module 5   Writing Complex Sentences Correctly

When finishing the learning of this module,

Goal 1   I will be able to write complex sentences.

Goal 2   I will learn to use noun clauses properly.

Goal 3   I will be able to distinguish attributive clauses from appositive clauses.

Section 1   Writing a Good Sentence

TASK ONE

Writing Complex Sentences

ACTIVITY ▶

Learning to write complex sentences

Step 1

Work in pairs. Underline dependent clauses in the following sentences.

1. Where they will hold the conference hasn't been announced.

2. Whether the servants will be sent to take care of the new-born baby is still a problem.

3. He didn't know what kind of fruits she liked.

4. The news that Mr. Lee will be fired because of the scandal is shocking.

5. This is how the child drives his parents crazy.

6. I don't know the tall beautiful woman who is dancing with him.

7. I have to go home to help my parents with the farming, which is a routine in every autumn.

8. As is reported, the president will visit the royal family and exchange ideas on the celebration of National Day.

9. It is believed that the Maori people came from the Pacific islands of Polynesia.

10. She is not what she was a few years ago.

11. I've got a feeling that one day the young actor will be successful.

12. Give him the letter as soon as he arrives at the hall.

13. No sooner had she opened the box than he came in.

14. The naughty girl didn't finish her homework until her father came back home.

15. I will not change my mind unless you agree to give me a copy of the textbook.

Step 2

Work in pairs again and identify the types of the dependent clauses you have found in each of the sentences given in Step 1.

Step 3

Rewrite the sentences in Step 1 by expressing the same ideas in sentences of different structures. Include dependent clauses in your sentences.

1. _____

2. _____

3. _____

4. _____

5. _____

6. _____

7. _____

8. _____

9. _____

10. _____

11. _____

12. _____

13. _____

14. _____

15. _____

TASK TWO

Using Noun Clauses in Writing

ACTIVITY ▶

Learning to write noun clauses properly

Step 1

Highlight the noun clause in each sentence below and underline the conjunction, conjunctive pronoun or conjunctive adverb in each noun clause. The first one is done as an example.

1. That everything in the world changes is often a theme in poetry.

2. Whether he comes to our party is still uncertain.

3. Who the letter was from is still unknown.

4. Whichever of you gets here first will get the prize.

5. Why they suddenly disappeared still remains a mystery.

6. It is believed that the old man takes great risk to go travelling by himself.

7. It seems that there are people from all over the world living here.

8. Another important difference is whether schools are state schools or private schools.

9. The problem is who will take charge of this shop.

10. This is not what he told the police.

11. This is when I realized the importance of being a journalist.

12. I asked her whether she had looked at a map yet.

13. I'll just say whatever comes into my mind.

14. The problem that economics is getting worse seems to be quite serious.

15. You have to answer my question whether you can lend me your book.

Step 2

Work in pairs and figure out the specific type of noun clause you found in each sentence in Step 1.

Step 3

Work in pairs. Make a diagram to classify the noun clauses and the conjunctions, conjunctive pronouns or conjunctive adverbs used in noun clauses, based on your work done in Steps 1 and 2.

Step 4

Work in pairs and make sentences with different types of noun clauses included in the sentences, and with conjunctions, conjunctive pronouns or conjunctive adverbs used properly.

Step 5

Work in pairs and analyze the uses of "that" in noun clauses in the following sentences.

1. That the football player will visit our city has been widely reported.
2. My plan is that two of you form a group and finish the task together.
3. The thought came to the general that maybe the enemy had changed their route.
4. I think (that) one day he will understand why his parents want him to major in Financial Management.
5. They share little in common except that they are from the same country.
6. I believe (that) you've done your best and that things will improve.

> **Summarize the uses of "that" in noun clauses**

Step 6

Work in pairs and analyze the following sentences. Figure out the differences between the uses of "whether" and "if" in noun clauses.

1. Whether the professor will deliver the speech hasn't been decided.
2. The point is whether you make progress when you have to balance work with family life.
3. We had some doubt whether she could hand in the paper in time.
4. The message doesn't say whether/if the lecture will be delayed.
5. That depends on whether you are suitable for the job.
6. I don't know whether she will come or not.

Summarize the differences between the uses of "whether" and "if" in noun clauses

TASK THREE
Distinguishing Attributive Clauses from Appositive Clauses

ACTIVITY ▶

Identifying similarities and differences

Step 1

Work in groups of 3-4 members. Highlight the attributive clauses and underline the appositive clauses in the following sentences.

1. The news that our national basketball team won the game encouraged us a lot.

2. The fairy is a little girl who has magic power.

3. I've come from Mr. Zhang with a message that he won't be about to see you tomorrow.

4. The school shop, whose customers are mainly students, has been closed since the end of the semester.

5. This is the student who won the first place last month.

6. The thought came to her that she might leave her key on the table when she came out this morning.

7. Where did you get the idea that the old man would not come?

8. She has a gift for creating an atmosphere for her students which allow them to express their ideas freely.

9. Word comes that China will launch its new manned spaceship this summer.

10. The first letter that I got from my friends will be kept.

Step 2

Work in groups and summarize the differences and similarities between attributive clauses and appositive clauses.

ASSIGNMENTS

Learn grammar about adverbial clauses:

1. Different types of adverbial clauses;
2. The linking words/subordinating conjunctions commonly used in adverbial clauses.

Module 6   Writing Attributive and Adverbial Clauses Correctly

When finishing the learning of this module,

Goal 1   I will be able to use attributive clauses properly.

Goal 2   I will be able to use adverbial clauses properly.

Goal 3   I will be able to avoid shifted constructions in writing.

Goal 4   I will be able to avoid run-on sentences in writing.

Section 1   Writing a Good Sentence

TASK ONE

Writing Attributive Clauses Correctly

ACTIVITY ▶

Understanding and writing different types of attributive clauses

Step 1

Work individually. Highlight the restrictive attributive clauses and underline the non-restrictive attributive clauses in the following sentences.

1. The place that I visited last summer is just the place where I spent my childhood.

2. The president of the World Bank says he has a passion for China，which he remembers starting as early as his childhood.

3. This is one of the best films that have ever been shown this year.

4. There is no simple answer, as is often the case in science.

5. I'm going to the airport to meet my uncle tomorrow morning, when he will be back from abroad.

6. The reason why he refused to attend the meeting was that they didn't give him an invitation earlier.

7. The newly-built café, the walls of which are painted light green, is really a peaceful place for us, especially after hard work.

8. American women usually identify their best friend as someone with whom they can talk frequently.

9. The place which interested me most was the Girls' Palace.

10. Do you know the year when the Chinese Communist Party was founded?

Step 2

Work in groups of 3-4 members and discuss the uses of restrictive attributive clauses and non-restrictive attributive clauses.

Step 3

Work individually and make five sentences with restrictive attributive clauses included and five sentences with non-restrictive attributive clauses included in the sentences.

1. _____

2. _____

3. _____

4. _____

5. _____

6. _____

7. _____

8. _____

9. _____

10. _____

Step 4

There is one mistake in each of the following sentences. Work in your group again, correct the mistakes and summarize the uses of relative pronouns in attributive clauses.

1. She told me everything which she knew.
2. This is the best novel which I have ever read.
3. Australia is the only country which is also a continent.
4. They talked of things and persons which they remembered in school.
5. Who is the girl which is talking to Tom in English?
6. A zoo is a park in that many kinds of animals are kept for exhibition.
7. Crusoe's dog, that was very old, becomes ill and died.
8. Let me show you the novel which I borrowed from the library which was newly open to us.
9. What's that that she is looking at?
10. You may take as many pens which you want.

Summarize the uses of relative pronouns in attributive clauses

TASK TWO

Writing Adverbial Clauses Correctly

ACTIVITY ▶

Learning to write adverbial clauses correctly

Step 1

Work individually. Underline the subordinating conjunctions used in each of the following sentences and translate the sentences into Chinese. The subordinating conjunction used in the first sentence is underlined as an example.

1. You'd better take the keys in case I'm out.

2. We spoke quietly for fear of waking the guards.

3. It's ten years since he smoked.

4. It may be many years before the situation improves.

5. He left before I could say anything.

6. Happy as they were, there were something missing.

7. While Tom's very good at science, his brother is absolutely hopeless.

8. Can you spare five minutes when it's convenient?

_____

9. We thought that, since we were in the area, we'd stop by and see them.

_____

10. People think I'm satisfied just because I don't complain.

_____

11. I sleep with the window open unless it's really cold.

_____

12. Wait until I come back.

_____

13. I remembered her name immediately she'd gone.

_____

14. No sooner had she said it than she burst into tears.

_____

15. I give you a map so you will not get lost.

_____

Step 2

Work in groups of 3-4 members and figure out the types of adverbial clauses in sentences in Step 1.

Step 3

Work individually and make 15 sentences with proper use of every subordinating conjunction you have found in Step 1.

1. _____

2. _____

3. _____

4. _____

5. _____

6. _____

7. _____

8. _____

9. _____

10. _____

11. _____

12. _____

13. _____

14. _____

15. _____

TASK THREE

Avoiding Shifted Constructions and
Run-on sentences in Writing

ACTIVITY ▶

Identifying the two sentence errors and making proper corrections

Step 1

Work in groups of 3-4 members. Analyze the underlined shifted constructions in the following sentences, and repair the sentences in the spaces provided

Types of Shifted Constructions	Examples
①Verb Tense	She caught the ball and then throws it to the catcher for the out.
②Voice	When the children turned on the TV, a buzzing sound was heard.
③Mood	Take two aspirins, and then you should call me in the morning.
④Person	If someone wants to play games, you must follow the rules.
⑤Number	When someone calls, tell them that I'm not at home.
⑥Discourse	My instructor asked whether I was prepared for the course and have I bought myself a laptop.

Step 2

Work in your group and discuss the following questions.

1. What is a shifted construction?
2. How should we avoid shifted constructions when writing sentences?

Step 3

Work in your group again and figure out the problems in the following run-on sentences.

1. The girls played basketball the boys played tennis.
2. Einstein is famous for $E=mc^2$ Edison is famous for the invention of the light bulb.
3. Titanic is my favorite movie I love eating popcorn.
4. Americans shake hands when they meet the Japanese bow.
5. Mother's Day is always on a Sunday Thanksgiving is always on a Thursday.
6. William loved visiting Montreal Sally preferred just to stay in Quebec.
7. My car broke down I need to buy a new one.
8. At one time few people had enough money to buy books few people could read books.
9. I want to learn Korean Trudy wants to learn Turkish.
10. People love peace they hate war.

Step 4

There is more than one way to correct run-on sentences. Please try different ways to correct the mistakes in the sentences given in Step 3, and rewrite the sentences.

1. _____

   _____

   _____

   _____

2. _____

_____

_____

_____

3. _____

_____

_____

_____

4. _____

_____

_____

_____

5. _____

_____

_____

_____

6. _____

_____

_____

_____

7. _____

_____

_____

_____

8. _____

_____

_____

_____

9. _____

_____

_____

_____

10. _____

_____

_____

_____

ASSIGNMENTS

Learn grammar about modal verbs and subjunctive and summarize：

1. The uses of different modal verbs；
2. Structures of sentences with different uses of subjunctive mood.

Module 7   Writing Compound-Complex Sentences Correctly

When finishing the learning of this module,

Goal 1   I will be able to write compound-complex sentences correctly.

Goal 2   I will know the uses of different modal verbs.

Goal 3   I will learn to use subjunctive mood properly.

Goal 4   I will be able to avoid misplaced modifiers in writing.

Goal 5   I will be able to avoid dangling modifiers in writing.

Section 1   Writing a Good Sentence

TASK ONE

Writing Compound-Complex Sentences

ACTIVITY ▶

Learning to write compound-complex sentences correctly

Step 1

Read the information box below.

Compound-Complex Sentences

A compound-complex sentence is made up of two or more independent clauses and one or more dependent clauses.

Step 2

Work individually. Read the following compound-complex sentences. Highlight the dependent clauses and underline the independent clauses.

1. Although I like to go camping, I haven't had the time to go lately, and I haven't found anyone to go with.

2. Sarah cried when her dog got sick, but she soon got better.

3. We decided that the movie was too violent, but our children, who like to watch scary movies, thought that we were wrong.

4. If Barack Obama is re-elected this November, he'll serve another four years, but it won't be an easy contest to win.

5. Even though he prefers to eat with a fork, he chooses to use chopsticks in Chinese restaurants; however, they aren't easy to use.

6. When I grow up, I want to be a pianist, and my mom is proud of me.

7. I usually use a pick whenever I play the guitar, or I just use my fingers.

8. His blue eyes were light, bright and sparkling behind half-mooned spectacles, and his nose was very long and crooked, as though it had been broken at least twice.

9. The door of the morning room was open as I went through the hall, and I caught a glimpse of Uncle Tom messing about with his collection of old silver.

10. All of us are egotists to some extent, but most of us—unlike the jerk—are perfectly and horribly aware of it when we make assess of ourselves.

11. Those are my principles, and if you don't like them . . . well, I have others.

12. The Druids used mistletoe in ceremonies of human sacrifice, but most of all the evergreen became a symbol of fertility because it flourished in winter when other plants withered.

13. We operate under a jury system in this country, and as much as we complain about it, we have to admit that we know of no better system, except possibly flipping a coin.

14. She gave me another of those long keen looks, and I could see that she was again asking herself if her favorite nephew wasn't steeped to the tonsils in the juice of the grape.

15. For in the end, freedom is a personal and lonely battle; and one faces down fears of today so that those of tomorrow might be engaged.

Step 3

Work individually and make five compound-complex sentences.

1. _____

2. _____

3. _____

4. _____

5. _____

Step 4

Find at least three students in your class and share your work in Step 3 with each of them.

TASK TWO

Using Modal Verbs Properly

ACTIVITY ▶

Learning to use modal verbs properly

Step 1

Work in pairs. Match each of the following functions of modal verbs with the sentences in which the modal verb(s) show the function(s) listed.

A. Indicating ability/lack of ability

B. Indicating possibility/impossibility

C. Asking/Giving permission

D. Indicating formal permission/prohibition

E. Making suggestion

F. Indicating an expectation or prediction that something will happen

G. Indicating necessity or requirement

1. He can't see you right now. He's in surgery.

2. Lisa can't speak French.

3. Can you lend me ten dollars? Yes, you can.

4. You may start your exam now.

5. The proposal should be finished on time.

6. You must have a passport to cross the border.

7. You may as well come inside. John will be home soon.

Step 2

Work in pairs and translate the following sentences into Chinese. Pay attention to the underline words.

1. May I come in?

_____

2. Her grandpa may well be over eighty.

_____

3. You may as well give him the letter.

_____

4. He can't be in the office, for the light has been turned off.

_____

5. You must be joking!

_____

6. I must have forgotten to tell you.

_____

7. He couldn't possibly have said why.

_____

8. We feel you <u>should not have done</u> that.

_____

9. We <u>needn't have hurried</u>, as we had plenty of time.

_____

10. It seems unfair that this <u>should</u> happen to me.

_____

Step 3

Work in a group of two pairs and check your answers together.

Step 4

In the same group, discuss the functions and meanings of the modal verbs in the sentences given in Step 2.

TASK THREE
Using Subjunctive Mood Properly

ACTIVITY ▶

Learning to use subjunctive mood properly

Step 1

Practice the following dialogue with a partner, and analyze the underlined parts to figure out when subjunctive mood should be used.

Peter: Hi, Marry! You look very upset. What's wrong with you?

Mary: Well, it's a long story. I am really in a bad mood.

Peter: Maybe I can help you, if you don't mind telling me.

Mary: It's just about the school hiking society. My parents don't want me to go hiking with the society because they always explore challenging... or even dangerous hiking trails.

Peter: Oh, but you work so hard to be admitted into the society. If I were you, I would talk with them, and I would show them my hiking plan and all the preparation I made.

Mary: It doesn't work at all! I wish they could be less worrying and more understanding.

Peter: Think about that... If you were a parent, would you be so understanding and supportive?

Mary: Well, I know what you mean. But my parents treat me as if I were a child. They always expect me to be confident and independent. I really doubt that. If they hoped so, they would not be so worrying.

Peter: Come on! Don't be upset. Parents also need time to be wonderful parents. Give them some time. Maybe you can take them to go hiking.

Mary: Maybe I can give it a shot. Anyway, thank you very much.

Peter: You're welcome.

Your answer: Subjunctive mood is used when _____

_____

_____

_____

_____

_____

Step 2

Work in pairs and discuss more uses of subjunctive mood. You may refer to the section "Direct Speech or Indirect Speech" in your speaking class.

TASK FOUR
Avoiding Misplaced or Dangling Modifiers in Writing

ACTIVITY ▶

Identifying the two sentence errors and making corrections

Step 1

Work in pairs. Analyze the following example and figure out the problem with the misplaced modifier in the example. (✕ means "Incorrect"; √ means "Correct".)

Example:
✕ On her way home, Jan found a *gold man's* watch.
√ On her way home, Jan found a *man's gold* watch.

- **What is wrong?**

Step 2

Correct the misplaced modifiers in the following sentences.

1. The child ate a cold dish of cereal for breakfast this morning.

2. The torn student's book lay on the desk.

3. Just John was picked to host the program.

4. We ate the lunch that we had brought slowly.

5. I only contributed $10 to the fund for orphaned children.

_____

6. The dealer sold the car to the buyer with leather seats.

_____

7. The three bankers talked quietly in the corner smoking pipes.

_____

8. They saw a fence behind the house made of barbed wire.

_____

9. I nearly made fifty dollars today.

_____

10. The waiter served a dinner roll to the woman that was well buttered.

_____

Step 3

Work in pairs. Analyze the example and figure out the problem with the dangling modifier in the example. (✕ means "Incorrect"; √ means "Correct".)

Example:

✕ *When nine years old*, my mother enrolled in medical school.

√ *When I was nine years old*, my mother enrolled in medical school.

• **What is wrong**?

Step 4

Correct the dangling modifiers in the following sentences.

1. Leaving quickly, my car lights were left on.

2. To complete a degree in anthropology, at least two history courses must be taken.

3. Carrying twenty-pound packs on our backs, the trail seemed very difficult.

4. In selecting her next car, cost had to be considered by Linda.

5. Comparing the totals carefully, discrepancies were found by the auditors.

6. While exercising at the gym, my shirt tore.

7. Originally written for children, many adults have enjoyed *Peter Pan*.

8. As the senior member present, the control panel was operated by Ms. Patton.

9. Protected by bubble wrap, anyone can ship this lamp anywhere.

10. After assaulting several bystanders, the police captured the criminal.

ASSIGNMENTS

Learn grammar about direct and indirect speech and subjunctive mood:

1. Grammar about direct and indirect speech
    a. When should direct speech and indirect speech be used?
    b. How can we convert speech from direct to indirect or vice versa?
    c. What should be noticed about tenses and punctuation in the conversion?
2. Grammar about subjunctive mood
    a. What are the structures of subjunctive mood in if-clauses?
    b. What are the structures of subjunctive mood in sentences with *wish*, *as if*, *as though* and *only if*?

Module 8　Using Direct or Indirect Speech Properly

When finishing the learning of this module,

Goal 1　I will be able to use direct speech and indirect speech properly.

Goal 2　I will be able to use subjunctive mood correctly.

Goal 3　I will be able to avoid mixed constructions in writing.

Section 1　Writing a Good Sentence

TASK ONE

Practicing Writing Compound-Complex Sentences

ACTIVITY ▶

Using compound-complex sentences properly

Step 1

Translate the following sentences into English. Make two translations for each sentence.

1. 虽然今年夏天天气炎热,但他整个暑假都在跑步,而且他还每周去两次健身房。

_____

_____

2. 他天赋异禀,又非常勤奋,人们都相信他将来能在画画上有所成就。

_____

_____

3. 据说因为定价不合理,这家商场没营业几天就倒闭了,还好我没在那里买什么东西。

_____

_____

4. 由于设备和场地存在安全隐患,演唱会被临时取消了,歌迷们都非常郁闷。

_____

_____

5. 她整个学期都在准备毕业演唱会,所以几乎没怎么为期末考试做准备,考试成绩不理想也在意料之中。

_____

_____

TASK TWO
Using Direct Speech and Indirect Speech Properly

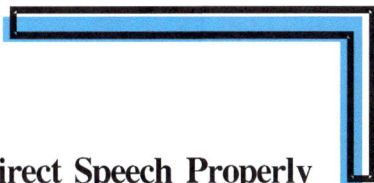

ACTIVITY 1 ▶

Understanding the use of direct and indirect speech

Step 1

Read the information box below.

Direct or Indirect Speech?
Both terms describe a way of **recounting** something that may have been said, but there is a subtle difference between them.

Direct speech describes when something is being repeated exactly as it was, usually in between a pair of inverted commas.
For example: She told me, **"I'll come home by 10 p. m."**

Indirect speech will still share the same information. But instead of expressing someone's comments or speech by directly repeating them, it involves reporting or describing what was said. An obvious difference is that with indirect speech, you won't use inverted commas.

For example: She said to me **that she would come home by 10 p. m.**

Step 2

Work in groups of 3-4 memebrs and discuss when the two types of speeches are used in your life.

ACTIVITY 2 ▶

Understanding the usages of direct speech and indirect speech

Step 1

Since the two types of speech are used to recount or report others' words, verbs like "tell" and "say" are called <u>reporting verbs</u> in direct speech and <u>reported verbs</u> in indirect speech. Please write five reporting/reported verbs except "tell" and "say".

Write five reporting/reported verbs

Step 2

Read the following examples. Work in groups and summarize how to convert direct speech into indirect speech.

She said, "It's hot here."	She said it was hot there.
She said, "I'm teaching French online."	She said she was teaching French online.
She said, "I've been on the web since 1996."	She said she had been on the web since 1996.
She said, "I've been teaching German for seven years."	She said she had been teaching German for seven years.
She said, " What shall we learn today?"	She asked what we should learn that day.
She said, "I was teaching earlier."	She said she had been teaching earlier.
She said, " The lesson had already started when he arrived."	She said the lesson had already started when he arrived.
She said "I'll teach English online tomorrow."	She said she would teach English online the next day.
She said, "May I open a new browser?"	She asked if she might open a new browser.

Summarize how to convert direct speech into indirect speech

Step 3

Work individually and convert the following direct speech into indirect speech, and change indirect speech into direct speech.

1. Clinton said, "I am very busy now."

   _____

2. He said, "My mother is writing letter."

   _____

3. He said, "I have passed the examination."

   _____

4. "Have you finished your homework?" Tom's mother asked him.

   _____

5. He said, "What a beautiful day!" (*Use two ways to convert.*)

   _____

   _____

6. John said, "You should take a holiday."

   _____

7. They complained that the homework was too much.

   _____

8. He said that he could be responsible for their actions.

   _____

9. He told me that this would be the last chance to meet the football player.

   _____

10. She screamed that he was crazy.

   _____

TASK THREE

Using Subjunctive Mood Correctly

ACTIVITY 1 ▶

Understanding the uses of subjunctive mood

Step 1

Work in groups of 3-4 members. Summarize the tenses that can be used in complex sentences with subjunctive mood used in if-clauses, and fill up the form following the sentences given below.

1. If I were a butterfly, I would have wings.

2. If he were to bring Martha to Hainan for the honeymoon, she might be upset.

3. If he were more diplomatic, he would make a better leader.

4. If I had more free time, I would go to see him more often.

5. If I were you, I wouldn't pay too much attention to them.

6. If you had listened to my advice, you would not have been in the trouble.

7. If I were in your position, I wouldn't do that silly thing.

8. Another thing is, if you should come to Brunei, you would take off your shoes before going into someone's house.

9. If they had known their neighbor was a drummer, they wouldn't have moved into the building.

10. He wouldn't have had that accident if he had been careful.

Tense	If-clauses		Main Sentences/Clauses		
Future	If he		he	would, could, should, might	do
Present	If he		he		
Past	If he		he		

┌ ─ ─ ─ ─ ─ ─ ┐
Step 2
└ ─ ─ ─ ─ ─ ─ ┘

Work individually. Carefully study the examples below and fill in blanks with proper words or words in brackets in their proper forms.

Examples：

要是他参加聚会多好！ → If only he would join the party!

我真希望他当时来参加聚会！ → I wish he had joined the party!

现在看上去仿佛已经是春天了。 → It seems as if it were spring already.

警察坚持要看一眼。 → The policeman insisted that he should have a look.

1. If only I _____ ten years old.

2. If only she _____ ahead and _____ better (look, plan).

3. I wish you _____ help me.

4. I felt as if I _____ something wrong (do).

5. He talks as if he _____ everything (know).

6. They acted as if they _____ friends for years (be).

7. It's necessary that we _____ at least one foreign language (master).

8. My suggestion is that we _____ to cut back on production (try).

9. It's strongly recommended that the machine _____ checked every year (be).

10. The commission commanded that work on the building _____ (cease).

TASK FOUR
Avoiding Mixed Constructions in Writing

ACTIVITY 1 ▶

Identifying mixed constructions

Step 1

Work in groups of 3-4 members. Read the following examples, and summarize what a mixed construction is and how to correct mixed constructions in writing. (✕ means "Incorrect"; √ means "Correct".)

1. ✕ For most people who have pets live longer, happier lives.
   √ For most people who have pets, life is longer and happier.
   √ Most people who have pets live longer, happier lives.

2. ✕ The court decided that the woman's welfare was not safe with her abusive partner.
   √ The court decided that the woman was not safe with her abusive partner.

3. ✕ Doctors, an honorable profession, requires a great attention to detail and a lot of memorization.
   √ Medicine, an honorable profession, requires a great attention to detail and a lot of memorization.

4. ✕ In his attempt to win the election broke several rules about pre-poll publicity.
   √ In his attempt to win the election, the candidate broke several rules about pre-poll publicity.
   √ The candidate's attempt to win the election broke several rules about pre-poll publicity.

5. ✕ The new automated answering machine we began to use it in the fall.

    ✓ We began to use the new automated answering machine in the fall.

Step 2

Work individually and correct the mixed constructions in the following sentences. There is more than one way to improve each sentence.

1. The fact that strays were overrunning the town and creating a health problem and nuisance.

2. When minute, pellet-sized bar codes became available and created a radical alternative to neutering or destroying strays.

3. With the bar code implants, runaway cats could be identified and quickly returned to pet owners instead of being destroyed.

4. One sign of trouble was when animal rights groups protested the indignity of the solution and when comedians asked, "Are people next? "

5. Advanced, miniaturized technology used for instant identification breathes fear into those who vigilantly protect against invasions of privacy.

ASSIGNMENTS

Learn grammar about comparison and inversion, and summarize:

1. Different structures and uses of comparison in writing;
2. Differences between the sentence structures of partial inversion and full inversion.

Module 9   Writing Inverted Sentences Correctly

When finishing the learning of this module,

Goal 1   I will be able to write inverted sentences properly.

Goal 2   I will be able to avoid faulty comparison in writing.

Section 1   Writing a Good Sentence

TASK ONE

Analyzing and Writing Inverted Sentences

ACTIVITY 1 ▶

Understanding structures of inverted sentences

Step 1

Work in groups of 3-4 members. Change the following inverted sentences into normal sentences, and then summarize the basic structures of inverted sentences.

1. Here comes the old man.

2. Never will I forgive her.

3. There stood a cat before her.

4. Away went the woman.

5. At the foot of the mountain lies a beautiful lake.

6. Walking at the head of the line was our captain.

7. Not until I saw Tom with my own eyes did I believe he was still alive.

8. Hardly had I reached the airport when the plane took off.

9. Only by this means is it possible to explain the problem.

10. So loudly did she speak that people in the next room could hear her.

Note down the RESULTS of your discussion

Step 2

Discuss the following questions in your group.

1. Which sentences in Step 1 have full inversion? Which have partial inversion?
2. What are the differences in structures between full inversion and partial inversion?
3. When should we use partial inversion and full inversion?

Note down the RESULTS of your discussion

ACTIVITY 2 ▶

Learning to write inverted sentences

Step 1

Change the following normal sentences into inverted sentences.

1. I knew it only when she told me.

2. I didn't realize how much time I had wasted until I began to work.

3. We had no sooner reached home than it began to rain.

4. Two towns lie east of the lake.

5. A wounded soldier was lying under the tree.

6. The boss has seldom been so upset.

7. The situation was so strange that I couldn't sleep.

8. I have read little concerning nanotechnology.

9. I didn't think I would be offered the job, so I was amazed when I got it.

10. If I had known it would be so difficult, I would never have enrolled.

Step 2

Invert the following sentences, using words in brackets at the beginning of each.

1. I haven't ever felt so lonely. (never)

2. I couldn't work because of the loud noise. (so)

3. She didn't play a lot of basketball. (little)

4. Peter didn't understand the situation. If he had, he would have quit. (had)

5. The story hasn't been told correctly. (rarely)

6. She bought the car after he had explained its benefits. (only after)

7. I don't eat pork very often. (seldom)

8. I would have bought a new house if I had had enough money. (had)

9. I will sign the check when you finish the work. (only when)

10. It was a day that we will all remember forever. (such)

TASK TWO

Avoiding Faulty Comparison in Writing

ACTIVITY ▶

Identifying sentence errors and making corrections

Step 1

Review what you have learned in TASK TWO of Module 2.

Step 2

Work individually and translate the following sentences into English.

1. 他比他姐姐更努力。

   _____

2. 我比你大两岁。

   _____

3. 他在班里比任何一个别的学生都好。

   _____

4. 他越忙就越高兴。

   _____

5. 他无法跑得像你一样快。

   _____

6. 撒哈拉沙漠是世界上最大的沙漠。

   _____

7. 非洲是世界第二大陆。

   _____

Step 3

Work individually. Read the following sentences carefully and figure out the common mistakes in the sentences. (× means "Incorrect"; √ means "Correct".)

Examples：

1. × Blotto ice cream contains 50％ less fat.

   √ Blotto ice cream contains 50％ less fat than Dingo ice cream.

2. × The rugs at MacCall's department store are more expensive than Macy's.

   √ The rugs at MacCall's department store are more expensive than the rugs at Macy's.

3. ✕ Opinions of politicians are no more relevant than private citizens.

   ✓ Opinions of politicians are no more relevant than those of private citizens.

4. ✕ Jim works more slowly than anyone I know.

   ✓ Jim works more slowly than anyone else I know.

5. ✕ Tim always gave his sister more attention than his brother.

   ✓ Tim always gave his sister more attention than he gave his brother.

   ✓ Tim always gave his sister more attention than his brother gave to his sister.

Note down the RESULTS of your discussion

Step 4

Work in groups of 3-4 members and check your translation in Step 2. You can consult your teacher during your discussion.

Step 5

Correct the mistakes in the following sentences.

1. Megan sounds better than anyone we have heard.

2. I think it is more harder to understand Freud's theory than Watson.

3. During the Civil War, the North won more battles, which eventually led to the South's surrender.

4. Sophia's resume was more organized than Nick, but Nick's resume included more information.

5. Jan helped Dirk with his project more than Brandy on Saturday night.

ASSIGNMENTS

Learn grammar about pronouns and articles (the, a, an), and find out:

1. Correct uses of pronoun "it";
2. Correct uses of articles (the, a, an).

Module 10   Using Pronoun "It" and Articles Properly

When finishing the learning of this module,

Goal 1   I will be able to use pronoun "it" correctly.

Goal 2   I will be able to use articles correctly.

Goal 3   I will learn to use singular and plural forms accurately.

Section 1   Writing a Good Sentence

TASK ONE

Using Pronoun "It" Correctly

ACTIVITY ▶

Learning to use pronoun "it" correctly

Step 1

Match each of the usages of "it" with the proper sentence given below.

A. Used in specific sentence patterns

B. Used to represent specific things

C. Used to refer to distance, weather, climate, value and so on

D. Used to represent people, especially babies or persons you don't know who exactly they are

E. Used as a grammatical subject

F. Used as a grammatical object

Module 10 Using Pronoun "It" and Articles Properly

1. It's hard work, but I enjoy it.
2. Is it a boy or a girl?
3. It's high time you should go home.
4. It can be very hot in the summer here.
5. It's foolish of her to make such a decision in a hurry.
6. I think it best that you should stay.

Step 2

Make six sentences with different usages of "it" in your sentences.

1. _____
2. _____
3. _____
4. _____
5. _____
6. _____

Step 3

Work in groups of 3-4 members and share your work in Step 2.

Step 4

Find out problems in using "it" in the following sentences and improve the sentences.

1. It is honest for you to tell me the truth.

2. It is great importance to protect the environment.

3. It is clear they had no desire for peace.

4. It's illegal drive a car without a license.

5. It is no doubt that he will study abroad.

6. I find this difficult to remember so many grammars.

7. No matter where he is, he makes a rule to go for a walk before breakfast.

8. I hate so when the weather in Changsha becomes freezing cold because there is no heater inside.

9. The weather will be rainy.

10. That is Jane that cooks the dinner every day.

TASK TWO

Using Articles Correctly in Writing

ACTIVITY ▶

Understanding the uses of articles "the" "a" and "an"

Step 1

Work in groups of 3-4 members. Translate the following sentences and analyze the uses of "the" "a" and "an" in these sentences.

1. On Monday, an unarmed man stole $1,000 from the bank. The thief hasn't been caught yet.

2. The sun rose at 6:17 this morning.

3. This is the highest building in New York.

4. The French enjoy cheese.

5. He was born in the seventies.

6. This is the only day we've had sunshine all week.

7. They are travelling in the Arctic.

8. A plane is a machine that can fly.

9. There is a tree in my garden.

10. What a shame they couldn't come.

Step 2

Work in your group and figure out when definite article "the" and indefinite articles "a/an" should not be used, after reading the following sentences.

1. Germany is an important economic power.

2. French is spoken in Tahiti.

3. Lunch is my favorite meal.

4. John is coming over later.

5. Prince Charles is Queen Elizabeth's son.

6. His brother's car was stolen.

7. Engineering is a well-paid career.

8. I'll get the card at Smith's.

9. 1948 was a wonderful year.

10. Rice is an important food in Asia.

11. Mount McKinley is the highest mountain in Alaska.

12. Victoria Station is in the center of London.

Step 3

Work in your group and summarize the uses of "the" "a" and "an" in a table.

Step 4

Make seven sentences with article "the" of different uses.

1. _____

2. _____

3. _____

4. _____

5. _____

6. _____

7. _____

Step 5

Find out problems in using articles in the following sentences and improve them.

1. There is a position available in my team. A job will involve some international travel.

2. My father enjoyed a book you gave him.

3. An man who wrote this book is famous.

4. Clouds drifted across a sky.

5. A CEO of TOTAL is coming to our meeting.

6. She read a last chapter of her new book first.

7. An elderly require special attention.

8. This is a painting from 1820's.

9. You are an only person he will listen to.

10. The party was success.

TASK THREE

Using Nouns in Singular and Plural Forms Accurately in Writing

ACTIVITY ▶

Learning to use nouns in singular and plural forms accurately

Step 1

Work individually and write the plural forms of the following nouns. You can refer to dictionaries.

Singular	Plural
boat	
cat	

Singular	Plural
foot	
leaf	

Singular	Plural
bus	
box	
spy	
woman	
child	
sheep	

Singular	Plural
knife	
potato	
fungus	
analysis	
datum	
fish	

☺What do you learn about nouns in singular or plural forms in this step?

Step 2

Work individually and correct the mistakes in the following sentences.

1. The news are at 5:30 p. m.

2. Athletics are good for young people.

3. Linguistics are the study of language.

4. Darts are a popular game in England.

5. Billiards are played all over the world.

6. My trousers is too tight.

7. Her jeans is black.

8. Those glasses is his.

☺What do you learn about nouns in singular or plural forms in this step?

Step 3

Complete the following sentences with words given in brackets in their proper forms.

1. The worker and writer _____(be) from Wuhan.

2. The singer and the dancer _____(be) from Beijing.

3. Many a boy and girl _____(have) made the same mistake.

4. Reading is _____(a, the, 不填) great pleasure in life.

5. Three thousand miles _____(be) _____(a, the, 不填) long distance.

6. Not only his family but also he _____(like) Chaplin's movies.

7. The police _____(be) investigating the new case.

8. The old _____(be) taken good care of in our society.

9. The beautiful _____(be) not always the same as the good.

10. The army _____(be) going to remain in this town.

11. Jim was one of the boys who _____(be) late for class.

12. Jim was the only one of the boys who _____(be) late for class.

13. None of these people _____(be) teachers.

14. None of the money on the table _____(be) mine.

15. Two-fifths of the students in the class _____(be) from Arabic-speaking countries.

ASSIGNMENTS

Review and summarize what you have learned:

1. Knowledge about sentence writing
   - Elements in sentences
   - Sentence patterns
   - Sentence structures

2. Knowledge about grammar
   - Dependent clauses
   - Direct speech and indirect speech
   - Non-finite verbs
   - Subjunctive mood
   - Passive voice
   - Modal verbs
   - Pronouns
   - Articles

Module 11　Reviewing Sentence Writing

When finishing the learning of this module,

Goal 1　I will have a better understanding of key concepts in sentence writing.

Goal 2　I will have a better understanding of the grammar learned.

Goal 3　I will be able to use punctuation properly in English writing.

Section 1　Writing a Good Sentence

TASK ONE

Reviewing Key Concepts in Sentence Writing

ACTIVITY ▶

Reviewing what you have learned about sentence writing

Step 1

Review basic elements in sentences by making ten sentences with different basic elements included in the sentences.

Basic Elements of Sentences
- Subject (in different forms)
- Predicate (*vi.* , *vt.* , *link v.*)
- Object (direct, indirect)
- Predicative
- Appositive
- Complement

1. _____

2. _____

3. _____

4. _____

5. _____

6. _____

7. _____

8. _____

9. _____

10. _____

Step 2

Write down the five basic sentence patterns in English.

1. _____

2. _____

3. _____

4. _____

5. _____

Step 3

Write down the four types of sentence structures.

Sentence Structures
- Simple Sentence
- _____ Sentence
- _____ Sentence
- _____ Sentence

Module 11   Reviewing Sentence Writing

Read the following passage. Analyze the sentence patterns and the elements in the seven underlined sentences, and find out the structures of these sentences.

Why College Is Not Home

The college years are supposed to be a time for important growth in autonomy and the development of adult identity. (1) However, now they are becoming an extended period of adolescence, during which many of today's students are not shouldered with adult responsibilities.

(2) For previous generations, college was a decisive break from parental control; guidance and support needed to come from people of the same age and from within. In the past two decades, however, continued connection with and dependence on family, thanks to cell phones, E-mail and social media, have increased significantly. Some parents go so far as to help with coursework. (3) Instead of promoting the idea of college as a passage from the shelter of the family to autonomy and adult responsibility, universities have given in to the idea that they should provide the same environment as that of the home.

To prepare for increased autonomy and responsibility, college needs to be a time of exploration and experimentation. This process involves "trying on" new ways of thinking about oneself both intellectually and personally. While we should provide "safe spaces" within colleges, we must also make it safe to express opinions and challenge majority views. Intellectual growth and flexibility are fostered by strict debate and questioning.

Learning to deal with the social world is equally important. (4) Because a college community differs from the family, many students will struggle to find a sense of belonging. (5) If students rely on administrators to regulate their social behavior and thinking pattern, they are not facing the challenge of finding an identity within a larger and complex community.

Moreover, the tendency for universities to monitor and shape student behavior runs up against another characteristic of young adults: the response to being controlled by their elders. (6) If acceptable social behavior is too strictly defined and controlled, the insensitive or aggressive behavior that administrators are seeking to minimize may actually be encouraged.

It is not surprising that young people are likely to burst out，particularly when there are reasons to do so. Our generation once joined hands and stood firm at times of national emergency. (7) <u>What is lacking today is the conflict between adolescent's desire for autonomy and their understanding of an unsafe world.</u> Therefore，there is the desire for their dorms to be replacement homes and not places to experience intellectual growth.

Every college discussion about community values，social climate and behavior should include recognition of the developmental importance of student autonomy and self-regulation，of the necessary tension between safety and self-discovery.

Sentence (1)：

Sentence (2)：

Sentence (3)：

Sentence (4)：

Sentence (5)：

Sentence (6)：

Sentence (7)：

Step 5

Separate sentences (1)，(3)，and (7) into different simple sentences as shown in the following example.

Example：
Sentence (6) can be separated into three simple sentences：
- Acceptable social behavior is too strictly defined and controlled.
- The insensitive or aggressive behavior may actually be encouraged.
- Administrators are seeking to minimize the intensive or aggressive behavior.

Sentence (1)：

Sentence (3):

Sentence (7):

TASK TWO

Reviewing Grammar

ACTIVITY ▶

Reviewing what you have learned about grammar

Step 1

Make 10 sentences as required: four sentences with different types of noun clauses; two with attributive clauses; four with different types of adverbial clauses.

1. _____

2. _____

3. _____

4. _____

5. _____

6. _____

7. _____

8. _____

9. _____

10. _____

Step 2

Make five sentences with different forms of non-finite verbs used in the sentences.

1. _____

2. _____

3. _____

4. _____

5. _____

Step 3

Read the following short dialogues and change the direct speech into indirect speech. The first one has been done as an example.

1. Mary: Hi Peter. What are you doing?

   Peter: Hi Mary. I'm filling out a job application.

   —Mary said hi to Peter and asked what he was doing.

   —Peter replied that he was filling out a job application.

2. Mary: Are you finished with school already?

   Peter: No. I have one more semester, but it would be great to have a job lined up.

3. Mary: How is your day going?

   Peter: Quite busy. I'm preparing for my presentation tomorrow on our marketing strategy. I'm not even half done yet.

4. Mary：You must feel stressed out now.

　　Peter：That's an understatement.

5. Mary：What are you doing now?

　　Peter：I'm playing pool with my friends at a pool hall.

6. Mary：I didn't know you play pool. Are you having fun?

　　Peter：I'm having a great time. How about you? What are you doing?

7. Mary：I'm taking a break from my homework. There seems to be no end to the amount of work I have to do.

　　Peter：I'm glad I'm not in your shoes.

Step 4

Choose the best one from the four choices to complete each sentence below.

1. We _____ back in the hotel now if you didn't lose the map. （2014,北京卷）

　　A. are　　　　　B. were　　　　　C. will be　　　　D. would be

2. _____ no modern telecommunications，we would have to wait for weeks to get news from around the world. （2014,福建卷）

　　A. Were there　　　　　　　　B. Had there been

　　C. If there are　　　　　　　　D. If there have been

3. If Mr. Dewey _____ present，he would have offered any possible assistance to the people there. （2014,湖南卷）

　　A. were　　　　B. had been　　　　C. should be　　　D. was

4. We would rather our daughter _____ at home with us，but it is her choice，and she is not a child any longer. （2014,陕西卷）

　　A. would stay　　B. has stayed　　　C. stayed　　　　D. stay

5. _____ the morning train，he would not have been late for the meeting. （2014,天津卷）

　　A. Did he catch　　　　　　　　B. should be catch

　　C. has he caught　　　　　　　　D. Had he caught

6. They were abroad during the months when we were carrying out the

093

investigation, or they _____ to our help. (2014,浙江卷)

　　A. would have come　　　　　B. could come

　　C. have come　　　　　　　　D. had come

7. It was John who broke the window. Why are you talking to me as if I _____ it? (2014,重庆卷)

　　A. had done　　　　　　　　B. have done

　　C. did　　　　　　　　　　　D. am doing

8. —It rained cats and dogs this morning. I'm glad we took an umbrella.

　　—Yeah, we would have got wet all over if we _____. (2013,重庆卷)

　　A. hadn't　　　B. haven't　　　C. didn't　　　D. don't

9. I _____ to my cousin's birthday party last night, but I was not available. (2013,安徽卷)

　　A. went　　　　　　　　　　B. had gone

　　C. would go　　　　　　　　D. would have gone

10. Harry is feeling uncomfortable. He _____ too much at the party last night. (2013,辽宁卷)

　　A. could drink　　　　　　　B. should drink

　　C. would have drunk　　　　D. must have drunk

11. I love the weekend, because I _____ get up early on Saturdays and Sundays. (2016,北京卷)

　　A. needn't　　B. mustn't　　C. wouldn't　　D. shouldn't

12. I was really annoyed; I _____ get access to the data bank you had recommended. (2016,天津卷)

　　A. wouldn't　　B. couldn't　　C. shouldn't　　D. needn't

13. You _____ be careful with the camera. It costs! (2015,四川卷)

　　A. must　　B. may　　　C. can　　　　D. will

14. —Sorry, Mum! I failed the job interview again.

　　—Oh, it's too bad. You _____ have made full preparation. (2015,福建卷)

　　A. must　　B. can　　　C. would　　　D. should

15. _____ I have a word with you? It won't take long. (2014,北京卷)

　　A. Can　　B. Must　　　C. Shall　　　D. Should

16. It's generally accepted that _____ boy must learn to stand up and fight like _____ man. (2017,全国卷)

　　A. a; a　　B. a; the　　C. the; the　　D. a; 不填

17. Experts think that _____ recently discovered painting may be _____

Picasso. (2017,浙江卷)

A. the;不填　　B. a;the　　　　C. a;不填　　　　D. the;a

18. Dr. Peter Spence, _____ headmaster of the school, told us, "_____ fifth of pupils here go on to study at Oxford and Cambridge. "(2017,四川卷)

A. 不填;A　　B. 不填;The　　C. the;The　　D. a;A

19. In many years, the education system in the U.S. is not very different from _____ in the UK. (2016,浙江卷)

A. that　　　B. this　　　C. one　　　　D. it

20. The research group produced two reports based on the survey, but _____ contained any useful suggestion. (2015,福建卷)

A. all　　　B. none　　　C. either　　　D. neither

TASK THREE

Using Punctuation Correctly in Writing

ACTIVITY ▶

Learning to use punctuation correctly in writing

Punctuation in English

,	comma	A's	apostrophe
.	period/stop/full stop	!	exclamation point
:	colon	?	question mark
;	semi-colon	/	slash
-	hyphen	—	dash
( )	parentheses	{ }	braces
[ ]	square brackets	<>	angle brackets
" "	quotation marks	…	ellipses

Step 1

Work in groups of 3-4 members and summarize the uses of these punctuation according to the following examples.

1. "Any further delay," she said, "would result in a lawsuit. "

2. His latest story is titled "The Beginning of the End"; wouldn't a better title be "The End of the Beginning"?

3. She nonchalantly told us she would be spending her birthday in Venice (Italy, not California). (Unfortunately, we weren't invited.)

4. The hastily arranged meeting came on the heels of less-than-stellar earnings.

5. Only a third of Americans have a passport; the majority of Canadians have a passport.

6. Only a third of Americans have a passport: for most, foreign travel is either undesirable or unaffordable.

7. I don't particularly like the play "Who's Afraid of Virginia Woolf"? I didn't like it even when I worked at Yahoo! I especially didn't like it when I saw it at 5:00 a. m.

Step 2

Work in your group and discuss the different uses of some punctuation marks, such as comma and semi-colon, in Chinese and English.

Note down the RESULTS of your discussion

ASSIGNMENTS

Review what you have learned about the following common sentence errors and the ways to avoid/correct them.

1. comma splice
2. sentence fragments
3. shifted constructions
4. run-on sentences
5. misplaced or dangling modifiers
6. mixed constructions

Module 12　Identifying Problems in Word Use

When finishing the learning of this module,

Goal 1　I will be able to avoid common sentence errors in writing.

Goal 2　I will be able to identify problems in word use.

Section 1　Writing a Good Sentence

TASK ONE

Identifying and Correcting Common Sentence Errors

Common Sentence Errors

1. Subject-verb disagreement
2. Comma splice
3. Sentence fragments
4. Shifted constructions
5. Run-on sentences
6. Misplaced or dangling modifiers
7. Mixed constructions
8. Faulty comparisons

Module 12　Identifying Problems in Word Use

ACTIVITY ▶

Correcting common sentence errors

Step 1

Correct subject-verb disagreements in the following sentences.

1. Dr. Ford is one of the professors who seems distracted most of the time.

2. Have either Luis or his parents written to Angela?

3. Neither Luis nor his parents has the least bit interest in keeping in touch with her.

4. Everybody on this team try really hard to please the new coach.

Step 2

Correct comma splice in the following sentences.

1. Kimberly sat on the bleachers and cheered for the team, Tom watched her as he vigorously defended the goal.

2. The cat jumped from step to step, it gracefully landed with each jump.

3. The professor stated that he especially favors personally connected papers, these papers reflect the most emotion.

4. Anthony did not agree with the method he was taught, he found other means to solve the problem.

Step 3

Correct sentence fragments in the following paragraph.

Although women's college basketball in Connecticut is a marvelously entertaining and popular sport. It not hard to remember. When it was not so popular. Which is hard to believe. Only a few years ago, my friends and I to go to a women's basketball game. And we could get seats for free near center court. Especially on Sunday afternoons. Of course, that before names such as Rebecca Lobo, Jean Rizzotti, and Kara Wolters became household words. Lobo's book, *Home-Court Advantage*, which she wrote with her mother. A best-seller in Connecticut. If more than a couple of hundred fans showed up for a game. It was considered a big turnout. And games were played in practically silent gyms. Because the fans didn't care who won. Nowadays, it almost impossible to buy tickets to a women's game, and you can't get seats. Unless you know someone.

Step 4

Correct shifted constructions in the following sentences.

1. When I bake cookies relaxes me.

2. My appointment to director was the position I wanted.

3. Workers who were consulted regularly feel more committed to the company and had a lower rate of absenteeism.

4. Hamlet delayed because he is overwhelmed by the events of the past few days.

Step 5

Correct mistakes in the run-on sentences below.

1. Judy leads a charmed life she never seems to have a serious accident.

2. People already believed the precious metals to be divine so their use in money intensified its allure.

3. Coins were minted of precious metals the religious overtones of money were then strengthened.

4. These powerful leaders decided what objects would serve as money their backing encouraged public faith in the money.

Step 6

Correct misplaced or dangling modifiers in the following sentences.

1. My wife found a photograph in the attic that Smith had given to Jones.

2. The grass was covered by the snow that was creating a lush carpet of green.

3. While exercising at the gym, my shirt tore.

4. Originally written for children, many adults have enjoyed *Peter Pan*.

Step 7

Correct mixed constructions in the following sentences.

1. The purpose of the program allows a student to solve a quadratic equation interactively.

2. The reason for Smith's firing is because he lied in his employment application.

3. Stripping, sanding, and painting, I will turn this chest into a real treasure.

4. Although the swimmers practiced twice a day, lost their first six meets.

Step 8

Correct faulty comparisons in the following sentences.

1. Slavery in the United States was much worse than Europe.

2. Winter is the most coldest season of the year.

3. Students in Beijing have much more opportunities than other cities in China.

4. Mary thinks that John is not as qualified for the job.

TASK TWO

Identifying and Solving Problems in Word Use

ACTIVITY 1 ▶

Understanding collocations in word use

Step 1

Read the underlined parts in the sentences below to understand types of collocations in word use.

1. His <u>dream</u> has finally <u>come</u> true.
   } ($n. + v.$ collocation)
   主谓搭配

2. Please make sure that no further <u>problems</u> will <u>arise</u>.

3. The students are <u>making</u> great <u>progress</u>.
   } ($v. + n.$ collocation)
   动宾搭配

4. He finally <u>realized</u> his <u>dream</u>.

5. The company has <u>high expectation</u> of the product.

6. This is an <u>extremly difficult</u> task.

7. His <u>chess skill</u> is superb.

8. We'd like to <u>positively encourage</u> you to buy the stock.

9. I <u>deeply regret</u> the loss of your loved one.

(*adj.* + *n.* collocation)
(*adv.* + *adj.* collocation)
(*n.* + *n.* collocation)
(*adv.* + *v.* collocation)
偏正搭配

Step 2

Underline collocations in the following paragraphs and categorize them into different types, based on what you have learned in Step 1.

1. When I left university I made a decision to take up a profession in which I could be creative. I could play the guitar, but I'd never written any songs. Nonetheless I decided to become a singer-songwriter. I made some recordings but I had a rather heavy cold so they didn't sound good. I made some more, and sent them to a record company and waited for them to reply. So, while I was waiting to become famous, I got a job in a fast-food restaurant. That was five years ago. I'm still doing the same job.

Your Categorization of Collocations

2. My friend Beth is desperately worried about her son at the moment. He wants to enroll on a course of some sort but just can't make a decision about what to study. I gave Beth a ring and we had a long chat about it last night. She said he'd like to study for a degree but is afraid he won't meet the requirements for university entry. Beth thinks he should do a course in management because he'd like to set up his own business in the future. I agreed that that would be a wise choice.

Your Categorization of Collocations

ACTIVITY 2 ▶

Understanding and solving problems in word use

Step 1

Read the following examples and figure out proper ways to deal with different kinds of problems in word use.

Problem 1: Wrong Collocation

1. Wrong: The price of milk is too expensive.
   Edited: The price of milk is too high.

2. Wrong: She likes to drink powerful coffee.
   Edited: She likes to drink strong coffee.

3. Wrong: Technology is a pivotal role for students' learning.
   Edited: Technology plays a pivotal role in students' learning.

4. Wrong: Students want to study in a relax room.
   Edited: Students want to study in a relaxing room.

Problem 2: Redundancy

1. Wrong: If all of us cooperate together, we will succeed.
   Edited: If all of us cooperate, we will succeed.

2. Wrong: The accused was guilty of false misstatement.
   Edited: The accused was guilty of misstatement.

3. Wrong: It was the general consensus of opinion that we must go to the movie.
   Edited: It was the general opinion that we must go to the movie.

Problem 3: Vague Reference

1. Wrong: James is going to keep the dog in a kennel as soon as he gets one.
   Edited: James is going to keep the dog in a kennel as soon as he gets a kennel.

2. Wrong: Harold beat Ted when he was out of practice.
   Edited: Harold beat Ted when Ted was out of practice.

3. Wrong: When the bus reached the station, it was almost empty.
   Edited: When the bus reached the station, the station was almost empty.

Common Problems in Word Use

1. Wrong collocation

   Wrong collocations are word partners that sound unnatural or incorrect to native speakers.

2. Redundancy

   Redundancy means superfluity or using words or expressions with similar meanings at the same time in a sentence.

3. Vague reference

   Vague reference is a common problem in sentences where "this" "it" "which" or other such words don't refer clearly back to any one specific word or phrase, but a whole situation.

> **Step 2**

Work individually and correct the mistakes of wrong collocations in the following sentences. You can refer to your dictionaries.

1. I achieved much money for one-month work.

2. White paper can make a pleasurable feeling to students.

3. Schools should add appropriate numbers of vivid colors in students' textbooks.

4. I greatly regret the loss of your loved one.

5. You'll save time if you close your smart phone and concentrate on the lesson.

6. Some people don't have enough risks in life.

7. Children can participate in various activities to achieve better well-being.

8. Addiction to the Internet can have some unhealthy habits.

9. Before the introduction of a vaccine it was a major public health threat.

10. The solution of the problem is still under discussion.

Module 12   Identifying Problems in Word Use

Step 3

Work individually and identify one common mistake in word use in the following sentences.

1. Her handbag was square in shape.

2. Detectives search for the true facts in an investigation.

3. The consensus of opinion on the basic fundamentals created the shortest meeting of the year.

4. If you refer back to the day of March 18 at eight o'clock in the morning, you will recall seeing a woman wearing a dress that was red in color gather together her belongings before crossing the street.

5. Even though she had performed the operation a numerous number of times, she still reviewed the basic essentials each and every day.

6. The first priority appears to be to group together the children that live in close proximity to one another.

7. The local residents filled to capacity the new auditorium as they waited to hear the developer recount the past history of the archaeological site.

8. Advance planning can help avoid total destruction of a historical site.

9. Fruit at Winn Dixie may possibly be cheaper in cost than fruit at Publix, but nevertheless it is of poorer quality.

10. In my personal opinion, we should refer back to last year's budget to see how we postponed that expenditure until a later time.

Step 4

Work in groups of 3-4 members and discuss what the common mistake is in sentences in Step 3.

Step 5

Correct the mistakes in each sentence in Step 3, and rewrite the sentences.

1.

2.

3.

4.

5.

6.

7.

8.

9.

10.

Step 6

Work individually and identify the one common mistake in word use in the following sentences.

1. After putting the disk in the cabinet, Mabel sold it.
2. Take the radio out of the car and fix it.
3. If the fans don't buy all the peanuts, pack them away until the next game.
4. The supervisors told the workers that they would receive a bonus.
5. The candy dish was empty, but we were tired of eating it anyway.
6. The witness called the television station, but they didn't answer.

7. Although Ms. Smith was wealthy, she made poor use of it.

8. It says in the paper that the legislation was passed.

9. Mega telephoned Howard yesterday to explain why she had not attended the meeting the day before. This made Howard very angry.

10. I didn't attend the rally, which was very unpatriotic.

Step 7

Work in groups of 3-4 members and discuss what the common mistake is in sentences in Step 6.

Step 8

Correct the mistakes in each sentence in Step 6, and rewrite the sentences.

1.

2.

3.

4.

5.

6.

7.

8.

9.

10.

ASSIGNMENTS

Review what you have learned in previous modules and get ready for the periodical test. The score of this test will be included in your final score of this term.

SECTION

2

Writing a Good Paragraph (1)

Module 13　Basic Features of a Well-Developed Paragraph

When finishing the learning of this module,

Goal 1　I will know the basic elements and their different roles in a paragraph.

Goal 2　I will know the features of a well-developed paragraph.

Goal 3　I will be able to identify problems in paragraph writing.

Section 2　Writing a Good Paragraph (1)

TASK ONE

Identifying Basic Elements in a Paragraph

ACTIVITY ▶

Analyzing and identifying basic elements in a paragraph

Step 1

Read the following paragraphs carefully.

Paragraph 1

On July 16, 1969, the Apollo 11 spacecraft launched from the Kennedy Space Center in Florida. Its mission was to go where no human being had gone before—the moon! The crew consisted of Neil Armstrong, Michael Collins, and Buzz Aldrin. The spacecraft landed on the moon in the Sea of Tranquility, a basaltic flood plain, on July 20, 1969. The moonwalk took place the following day. On July 21, 1969, at precisely 10:56 EDT, Commander Neil Armstrong emerged from the Lunar Module and took his famous first step onto the moon's surface. He declared, "That's one small step for man, one giant leap for mankind." It was a monumental moment in human history!

Paragraph 2

Canada is one of the best countries in the world to live in. First, Canada has an excellent health care system. All Canadians have access to medical services at a reasonable price. Second, Canada has a high standard of education. Students are taught by well-trained teachers and are encouraged to continue studying at university. Finally, Canada's cities are clean and efficiently managed. Canadian cities have many parks and lots of space for people to live. As a result, Canada is a desirable place to live.

Paragraph 3

The weather in 1816 Europe was abnormally wet, keeping many inhabitants indoors that summer. From April until September of that year, "it rained in Switzerland on 130 out of the 183 days from April to September." (Phillips, 2006) Unlike today, one could not simply turn on a television or click through the Internet in order to entertain oneself. Instead, it was much more common for the educated people of the day to spend time reading, discussing well-known authors and artists of the day, playing at cards and walking in their gardens and walking paths.

Step 2

Work in pairs and discuss the following questions about the three paragraphs above.

1. What is the main idea of each paragraph? How do you get it?
2. What role does each underlined sentence play in each paragraph?
3. What kind of information is given in the rest sentences of each paragraph?
4. What role do the rest sentences play in each paragraph?

Step 3

Work in groups and summarize the types and roles of the sentences in a paragraph.

Type of Sentence	Location in a Paragraph	Role in a Paragraph
_____ Sentence		introducing the topic and the main idea of a paragraph
_____ Sentence		supporting the main idea expressed in the topic sentence with evidence, details, etc.
_____ Sentence		bringing the paragraph to an end

Basic Elements of a Paragraph
- Topic Sentence
- Developing Sentence
- Concluding Sentence

TASK TWO

Recognizing Basic Features of
A Well-Developed Paragraph

ACTIVITY ▶

Analyzing and understanding basic features of a well-developed paragraph

Step 1

Discuss in groups of 3-4 members and answer the following questions about the three paragraphs given in TASK ONE.

1. What is each paragraph about?
2. Are there any other topic(s) or main idea(s) introduced in each paragraph?
3. What is the relation between the topic sentence and the developing sentences?
4. What is the relation between the topic sentence and the concluding sentence?
5. In what order are the developing sentences arranged? Why?
6. How are the sentences connected in each paragraph? And why?
7. Is it necessary to have a concluding sentence in a paragraph? Why?
8. Are there any other ways to close a paragraph? What are they?

Step 2

Work in groups and summarize the features of a well-developed paragraph.

To my understanding, a well-developed paragraph should...

Module 13　Basic Features of a Well-Developed Paragraph

Read the following paragraphs and answer questions after the paragraphs.

Paragraph 1

I hate wet and rainy days. It rained a lot in 1816, a lot like every day; the weather in Europe was abnormally wet because it rained in Switzerland on 130 out of the 183 days from April to September. If I were Mary Shelley I might decide to write a book too. After all, it was the only thing you could do without TV or anything. She said that she "passed the summer of 1816 in the environs of Geneva... we occasionally amused ourselves with some German stories of ghosts... These tales excited in us a playful desire of imitation". So, people were stuck inside and bored. Mary Shelley decided to write a book because it was so awful outside. I can totally see her point, you know? I guess I would write a novel if there was nothing else to do.

Paragraph 2

I live in a house in west Provo. I like the view from our house. We have lived there since November. We also have a car that I like very much. We were in an accident a few months ago. We hit a deer that was crossing the street at night. I felt sorry for the deer, but it cost a lot of money to repair the car.

Paragraph 3

When I was growing up, one of the places I enjoyed the most was the cherry tree in the back yard. Behind the yard was an alley and then more houses. Every summer when the cherries began to ripen, I used to spend hours high in the tree, picking and eating the sweet, sun-warmed cherries. My mother always worried about my falling out of the tree, but I never did. But I had some competition for the cherries—flocks of birds that enjoyed them as much as I did and would perch all over the tree, devouring the fruit whenever I wasn't there. I used to wonder why the grown-ups never ate any of the cherries; but actually when the birds and I had finished, there weren't many left.

Questions

1. Are these paragraphs well-developed? What problems can you find in each of them?

2. Does each paragraph have a topic sentence and a concluding sentence?

3. Does each paragraph have one and only one topic and main idea?

4. Do all the sentences in each paragraph focus on the same topic and help to develop the same idea? Is there any shift of topic in these paragraphs?

5. Are there any irrelevant sentences in these paragraphs?

6. What can be done to improve these paragraphs?

Step 4

Discuss in pairs. Summarize what a well-developed paragraph should be like by completing the following sentences. Read the information box below before your discussion.

1. A good paragraph should be _____.

2. A good paragraph should be _____.

3. A good paragraph should be _____.

Features of a Well-Developed Paragraph

- **Unity**

  Being unified with all sentences focusing on the same one topic, and developing the one main idea expressed in the topic sentence

- **Coherence**

  Being coherent with all sentences being arranged in a proper order, expressing a fluent and logical flow of thought in the paragraph

- **Completeness**

  Being complete with a topic sentence, developing sentences and a concluding sentence

---

ASSIGNMENTS

Read the following paragraphs carefully. Find out problems in the paragraphs and make necessary improvements where necessary.

1. It is a fact that capital punishment is not a deterrent to crime. Statistics show that in states with capital punishment, murder rates are the same or almost the same as in states without capital punishment. It is also true that it is more expensive to put a person on death row than in life imprisonment because of the costs of maximum security. Unfortunately, capital punishment has been used unjustly. Statistics show that every execution is of a man and that nine out of ten are black. So prejudice shows right through.

2. Piranhas rarely feed on large animals; they eat smaller fish and aquatic plants. When confronted with humans, piranhas' first instinct is to flee, not attack. Their fear of humans makes sense. Far more piranhas are eaten by people than people are eaten by piranhas. If the fish are well-fed, they won't bite humans.

3. Most people consider piranhas to be quite dangerous; they are, except in two main situations, entirely harmless. Piranhas rarely feed on large animals; they eat smaller fish and aquatic plants. When confronted with humans, piranhas' instinct is to flee, not attack. There are two situations in which a piranha bite is likely. When a frightened piranha is lifted out of the water—for example, if it has been caught in a fishing net. When the water level in pools where piranhas are living falls too low. A large number of fish may be trapped in a single pool, and if they are hungry, they may attack anything that enters the water.

4. Although most people consider piranhas to be quite dangerous, they are, for the most part, entirely harmless. Piranhas rarely feed on large animals; they eat smaller fish and aquatic plants. When confronted with humans, piranhas' first instinct is to flee, not attack. Their fear of humans makes sense. Far more piranhas are eaten by people than people are eaten by piranhas. A number of South American groups eat piranhas. They fry or grill the fish and then serve them with coconut milk or tucupi, a sauce made from fermented manioc juices.

Module 14   Understanding Unity in a Paragraph

When finishing the learning of this module,

Goal 1   I will understand unity in a paragraph.

Goal 2   I will know more about topic sentence, developing sentence and concluding sentence.

Goal 3   I will be able to identify irrelevant sentences in a paragraph.

Section 2   Writing a Good Paragraph (1)

TASK ONE

Understanding Unity in a Paragraph Writing

ACTIVITY ▶

Identifying problems that make a paragraph not unified

Step 1

Read the following two paragraphs carefully and analyze the paragraphs as required in Step 2.

Paragraph 1

The poodle makes a perfect pet because poodles offer their owners a companionship for life, not to mention that they have a loveable personality. Poodles are sweet, smart, playful, and well-mannered and they love to be around people. They are always willing to lend their unquestionable love and loyalty when you need the most and they are yours for life. Apart from being a happy spirited dog and a great companion, the poodle is small and doesn't require a lot of room, so it is ideal for apartments or city settings. The poodle is suited to most environments and lifestyles; whether it be living in the suburbs or downtown, with one person or a couple, or even living with a family and children, the poodle fits right in. The poodle is a dog that warms your heart with its character. It becomes a part of your family no matter where you live and it can provide you with love and companionship that you won't want to do without. In fact, you can't ask for a better dog.

Paragraph 2

It is a fact that capital punishment is not a deterrent to crime. Statistics show that in states with capital punishment, murder rates are the same or almost the same as in states without capital punishment. It is also true that it is more expensive to put a person on death row than in life imprisonment because of the costs of maximum security. Unfortunately, capital punishment has been used unjustly. Statistics show that every execution is of a man and that nine out of ten are black. So prejudice shows right through.

Step 2

Work in pairs and complete the following tasks.

1. Find out the topic sentence of each paragraph.
2. Find out what other topics are mentioned or ideas are expressed in each paragraph.
3. Find out change(s) of topic(s) if there is any in each paragraph.
4. Underline the topic sentence and the concluding sentence in each paragraph.
5. Find out connection(s) between the first and the last sentence in each paragraph.
6. Decide which paragraph is unified and explain why the other one is not unified.

Step 3

Discuss the following questions in groups.

1. What is the role of the topic sentence in a paragraph?

2. Should there be a focus for all the sentences of a paragraph? Why?

3. What is the role of developing sentences in a paragraph?

4. What kind of information or idea should be expressed in developing sentences?

5. Should other topics or ideas be included in the paragraph? Why or why not?

6. What kind of sentences are irrelevant sentences in a paragraph?

7. What should be done with irrelevant sentences in a paragraph?

8. What is the role of a concluding sentence?

Step 4

Summarize things to notice in making a paragraph unified.

1. Make the topic sentence _____.

2. Make all the sentences _____.

3. Make the developing sentences _____.

4. Make the concluding sentence _____.

5. Irrelevant sentences and shift of topics should _____.

TASK TWO

Understanding Functions of Different Sentences in a Paragraph

ACTIVITY 1 ▶

Understanding the topic sentence in a paragraph

Step 1

Work in pairs. Read Paragraph 1 again and answer the following questions.

Paragraph 1

(1) The poodle makes a perfect pet because poodles offer their owners a

companionship for life, not to mention that they have a loveable personality. (2) Poodles are sweet, smart, playful, and well mannered and they love to be around people. (3) They are always willing to lend their unquestionable love and loyalty when you need the most and they are yours for life. (4) Apart from being a happy spirited dog and a great companion, the poodle is small and doesn't require a lot of room, so it is ideal for apartments or city settings. (5) The poodle is suited to most environments and lifestyles; whether it be living in the suburbs or downtown, with one person or a couple, or even living with a family and children, the poodle fits right in. (6) The poodle is a dog that warms your heart with its character. (7) It becomes a part of your family no matter where you live and it can provide you with love and companionship that you won't want to do without. (8) In fact, you can't ask for a better dog.

1. Which sentence is the topic sentence of this paragraph?
2. What kind of information is given in the topic sentence?
3. What basic elements must be included in a topic sentence?
4. What is the relation between the topic sentence and other sentences in the paragraph?

Topic Sentence in a Paragraph
- **Basic elements of a topic sentence**
  Topic: stating the subject matter clearly and briefly; showing what the paragraph is mainly about
  Controlling idea: expressing the main idea or opinion about the topic; indicating how the writer will develop the topic in the paragraph
- **Focus of the paragraph**: controlling the content and the development of the whole paragraph; supported by all the rest sentences in the paragraph; giving the paragraph direction and purpose

ACTIVITY 2 ▶

Understanding the developing and concluding sentences in a paragraph

Step 1

Analyze the sentences in Paragraph 1 and answer the questions below.

1. What is the controlling idea expressed in the topic sentence?
2. What kind of information or idea(s) are provided in Sentences (2) to (7)? For what purpose(s)?
3. Is there any difference in the roles of Sentences (2) and (3), and Sentences (6) and (7)? What is the difference and for what purpose(s)?
4. Is it necessary to have Sentence (8) as the last sentence of the paragraph? Why?

Step 2

Analyze the sentences in Paragraph 2 and answer questions below.

Paragraph 2

(1) It is a fact that capital punishment is not a deterrent to crime. (2) Statistics show that in states with capital punishment, murder rates are the same or almost the same as in states without capital punishment. (3) It is also true that it is more expensive to put a person on death row than in life imprisonment because of the costs of maximum security. (4) Unfortunately, capital punishment has been used unjustly. (5) Statistics show that every execution is of a man and that nine out of ten are black. (6) So prejudice shows right through.

1. Which sentence is the topic sentence of this paragraph?
2. What is the controlling idea expressed in the topic sentence?
3. Do Sentences (2) to (5) support and develop the controlling idea expressed in the topic sentence?
4. Are Sentences (2) to (5) about the same one topic? If not, what are the topics?
5. What are the relation(s) between Sentences (1) and (2), and Sentences (4) and (5)?
6. Does Sentence (6) conclude the paragraph properly? Why or why not?
7. Is this a unified paragraph? Why or why not?

Module 14　Understanding Unity in a Paragraph

Based on your discussion in Step 1 and Step 2, summarize the features of developing sentence(s) and concluding sentence(s) in a unified paragraph.

1. Developing sentence(s):
   - Focus on _____.
   - Develop and support _____.
   - No _____ included in the paragraph.
2. Concluding sentence(s):
   - Be related to _____.
   - Complete the paragraph by _____.

Developing Sentences in a Paragraph
- **Focusing** on the **topic** and the **controlling idea** expressed in the topic sentence
- **Developing** the controlling idea into a paragraph
- **Supporting** the controlling idea with related evidence, details, etc.
  - **Major developing sentences** expressing **supporting ideas** to support the topic sentence
  - **Minor developing sentences** providing **supporting details** to support the supporting ideas

Concluding Sentence(s) in a Paragraph
- Being directly **related to** the topic and the main idea
- Bringing the paragraph to an **end** to make the paragraph **complete**
- Making a conclusion, summary, suggestion, prediction, restatement, etc.
- Indicating transition from one paragraph to another (sometimes at the beginning of the next paragraph)

Find out problems that make the following paragraphs not unified.

1. Starbucks is a very popular coffee chain that started in Seattle. Today this company makes millions of coffee drinks per day, and many people consider

those drinks to be an essential part of life. Mayor Joe Schmo surely sounded great in his speech yesterday. I wonder if he likes to drink Starbucks coffee. I know the guys from the band Outkast like Starbucks. Starbucks is a really great way to start your day.

2. With the changes in their social role, women's position in the family has been improved as well. Husband and wife are now equal in the family. They cope with problems of daily life together and share the responsibilities of doing household chores and taking care of children. But in some families, you can still find wives are being busy with dinners, while husbands are comfortably sitting in armchairs reading newspapers or watching football games on TV.

3. Television has many harms. Since the television was invented, it has played an important part in people's life. It has turned the big world to a small one. People can see the same program at the same time around the world. But, as soon as television comes into common families, it also has many harms, especially for the children. For example, children spend too much time watching television. As a result, they cannot concentrate on their studies. What is worse, their eyesight becomes poorer. And they are often exposed to violence, which is harmful to their mental growth.

ACTIVITY 3 ▶

Identifying irrelevant sentences in a paragraph

Step 1

Each given topic sentence below is followed by several additional sentences. Cross off the sentences that are irrelevant or off-topic.

1. Topic sentence: The increasing number of car accidents is a serious problem.
   (1) The number of accidents last year increased 10% over the year before.
   (2) One cause is the great increase in the number of cars on the road.
   (3) Ownership of a car involves a lot of expense.
   (4) There should be fewer accidents if drivers were more careful.

(5) A car owner must have a license.

(6) Many drivers do not pay attention to the speed laws.

2. Topic sentence: There are many medicines for a cold, but few of them are effective.

(1) People often catch cold in the winter or spring.

(2) If you have a cold, your friends will suggest medicines that they say are good.

(3) Pharmacies have dozens of remedies for colds.

(4) A person with a cold feels very uncomfortable.

(5) Doctors doubt the value of these remedies.

(6) Doctors usually say that the most effective thing to do is to stay in bed, keep warm, and drink lots of liquids

(7) People often catch cold from contact with a person who has a cold.

Step 2

Go over the sentences in Step 1 again. Arrange the relevant sentences in proper order and add concluding sentences to make the paragraphs complete.

To Achieve Unity in a Paragraph

• All sentences should focus on the same one topic and one main idea.

• All developing sentences should develop and support the main idea.

• There should be no irrelevant sentence or change of topic in the paragraph.

ASSIGNMENTS

Identify irrelevant sentences in the following paragraphs.

1. Alfred Hitchcock

(1) With more than fifty feature films Alfred Hitchcock remains one of the most popular directors of all time. (2) Hitchcock's films draw heavily on both fear and fantasy. (3) He began directing in the United Kingdom. (4) They often portray innocent people caught up in circumstances beyond their understanding. (5) The movie *Rebecca*, which evokes the fears of a young bride, is a good example of this.

2. Doping

(1) Doping is the use of drugs to try to improve sports performance. (2) This practice is banned by sports federations throughout the world. (3) Athletes need to know which substances are banned in sport. (4) The uses of drugs during athletic festivals are evident. (5) Furthermore, they must make sure that any product or medication they take does not contain a prohibited substance.

3. Pope John Paul Ⅱ

(1) Pope John Paul reigned as pope of the Roman Catholic Church for almost 27 years until his death. (2) He was the first non-Italian pope since the 16th century. (3) During his reign, the pope traveled extensively, visiting over 100 countries, more than any of his predecessors. (4) Even in 1992 as he was diagnosed with Parkinson disease, he continued with his travels. (5) He maintained an impressive physical condition throughout the 1980s.

4. Michael Schumacher

(1) Everyone who is interested in Formula One races knows Michael Schumacher. (2) Statistically he is the greatest driver of all time. (3) He used a homemade kart built by his father, who managed the local karting track. (4) He is also the first and only German to win the drivers' championship. (5) Furthermore, Schumacher is the most notable and well-paid figure in the recent history of Formula 1.

5. Film Festivals

(1) Film festivals, such as the Cannes Film Festival, involve showing many films over a short period of time. (2) It is a competition of sorts between all the different films produced in a given year in a country or within a certain film genre. (3) This year's Oscar Awards were given in March. (4) Such an event doesn't only include full-length feature films. (5) It may also be two or three minutes pieces and documentaries.

6. Socializing Dogs

(1) The term socialization of dogs is used to describe how a dog learns to relate to people and other dogs. (2) This process begins even before the puppy's eyes are open. (3) Once the dog starts biting, it is very difficult to overcome. (4)

For most puppies, a mother who interacts well with humans is the best teacher. (5) Therefore most experts today recommend leaving puppies with their mothers until at least 8 to 10 weeks of age.

7. Apples

(1) There is an old saying, "An apple a day keeps the doctor away and helps losing weight." (2) In fact, studies have shown that a number of components in apples help the body to fight many diseases. (3) Apples are also a source of dietary fiber which helps digestion and promotes weight loss. (4) Blackberries and apples are a traditional duo for pies. (5) Unlike other snacks such as biscuits, raw apples contain almost zero fat and cholesterol.

8. Sweden

(1) The 19th century Sweden saw a significant population increase. (2) Consequently many people found themselves unemployed. (3) Unemployment resulted in poverty and massive emigration. (4) It is believed that between 1850 and 1910 more than one million Swedes moved to the United States alone. (5) Its neutrality during World War II had been disputed.

9. Tsunami

(1) Although often referred to as tidal waves, a tsunami is not a usual wave which is only much bigger. (2) People unaware of the danger may remain at the shore for collecting fish from the exposed seabed. (3) Instead it is an endlessly onrushing tide that forces its way through any obstacle. (4) Most of the damage is caused by the huge mass of water behind the initial wave front. (5) The sheer weight of water is enough to pulverize objects in its path, often reducing buildings to their foundations.

Module 15　Achieving Coherence in Paragraph Writing

When finishing the learning of this module,

Goal　I will know ways to achieve coherence in paragraph writing.

Section 2　Writing a Good Paragraph (1)

TASK ONE

Arranging Sentences in Proper Order

ACTIVITY ▶

Analyzing and learning the proper orders of sentences

Step 1

Read the following paragraphs carefully.

Paragraph 1

　　On one corner of my dresser sits a smiling toy clown on a tiny unicycle — a gift I received last Christmas from a close friend. The clown's short yellow hair, made of yarn, covers its ears but is parted above the eyes. The blue eyes are outlined in black with thin, dark lashes flowing from the brows. It has cherry-red cheeks, nose, and lips, and its broad grin disappears into the wide, white ruffle around its neck. The clown wears a fluffy, two-tone nylon costume. The left side of the outfit is light blue, and the right side is red. The two colors merge in a dark line that runs down the center of the small outfit. Surrounding its ankles and disguising its long black shoes are big pink bows. The white spokes on the wheels of the unicycle gather in the center and expand to the black tire so that the wheel somewhat resembles the inner half of a grapefruit. The clown and unicycle together stand about a foot high. As a cherished gift from my good friend Tran, this colorful figure greets me with a smile every time I enter my room.

Paragraph 2

Meeting an old friend unexpectedly always gives a pleasant surprise. It brings back to one's mind sweet memories of early childhood and school-days. We become nostalgic. We enjoy remembering the pranks of our childhood. Only last Sunday, I had such a pleasant experience. I went to the railway station to receive my brother who was coming from Bengaluru. The train was late by half an hour. I was walking about at the platform. I saw a young man staring at me. It appeared that I had seen him somewhere. However, I could recall nothing. I abandoned the thought and continued walking. But the man was trying to recollect something. I looked at him closely. Suddenly I recollected that we were class fellows fifteen years back when my father was posted in Calcutta. He was Akshat. How much he had changed! I approached him and said hesitantly, "Akshat!" He said, "Alok!" And we embraced each other. We were very pleased at this unexpected meeting. We asked about each other's career, families, etc. We talked a lot. We remembered our old friends and teachers. We enjoyed remembering our mischief about the good old days. Both of us were so changed. He is now a major in the army and I am a school teacher.

Paragraph 3

This world is full of people of different kinds. Some are sincere and passionate in their dealings and relationships, but many pretend to be sincere so long as they have some purpose to serve. As soon as their purpose is served they change their attitude. They behave like friends but they are not friends. They are with you so long as there is scope for enjoyment. The moment you are in trouble, the moment you are in need, they will turn their back upon you. They are the false friends. True friends are the people who will always stand by you through thick and thin. They are always ready to help. They may go to any extent to help their friend. A false friend is mean and selfish. He will show his care, love and concern for you so long as his interest is fulfilled. He will always admire and flatter you. He is never constant in his dealing. He will apparently show an enthusiastic interest in you, but he will soon feel tired of you when he finds no scope for any gain in this relationship. Such a man is changeable in nature. He should be avoided. Friendship with this kind of man is not good. He can never be trusted. If we commit the mistake of trusting him and confide any of our secrets in him, he will take it as a golden opportunity. He will exploit those secrets to gain profit for himself at the cost of others. So we should be very cautious in our choice of friends.

Step 2

Discuss in groups and answer the following questions about the paragraphs in Step 1.

1. What are the topic, the main idea, and the purpose of writing of each paragraph?
2. What are the topic sentence and the concluding sentence of each paragraph?
3. How are the sentences arranged in each paragraph? In what order?
4. How are the sentences connected in each paragraph?

Achieving Coherence by Arranging Sentences in Proper Order
   a. in time order (in paragraphs of process, narration, etc.)
   b. in spatial order (in paragraphs of description, exposition, etc.)
   c. in logical order (in paragraphs of cause & effect, argument, comparison & contrast, etc.)

Step 3

Re-arrange each of the following groups of sentences in proper order to form a logical sequence and to construct a coherent paragraph.

1. A. Such a man goes on working hard and even if he fails he is never downcast.
   B. It is therefore, the man who labors hard with a strong resolution and an unshaken will, who achieves success and makes his fortune.
   C. In turn failures make him all the more determined and resolute and he persists in his task till he attains the desired success.
   D. A man who possesses a strong will and firm determination finds all difficulties solved.
   E. To him there are a thousand ways open to steer clear of all dangers and difficulties.
      Your answer: _____

2. A. But sometimes, the persons of opposite nature also come closer, fall in each other's company by accident or out of ignorance, vitiating the above statement to some extent.

   B. If a man moves in the company of good, gentle and noble people, he is usually adjudged to be a gentleman.

   C. It is usual for a man to see company of those who possess tastes, tendencies and temperaments like his own.

   D. On the other side, if he keeps company with evil persons and bad characters, he is considered to be a man of bad character.

   E. Generally, the character and conduct of a person is gauged by the kinds of people he mixes and moves with.

   Your answer: _____

3. A. Most of the perishable foods are shipped by refrigerator ships.

   B. As the green bananas are loaded, a man watches closely the signs of yellow on them.

   C. The cool temperatures keep the bananas from getting ripe during the trip.

   D. They are placed in the refrigerated hold of the ship.

   E. Some foods such as bananas are shipped before they get ripe.

   F. Ripe bananas are poor travelers and even one ripe banana at the start of the trip can spoil a whole shipload of fruit.

   Your answer: _____

4. A. Whatever the reasons may be, the effects are disastrous leading to both physical and mental ailments like insomnia, hypertension and nervous breakdown etc.

   B. According to psychologists it is the result of fear due to inexperience, deprivation, isolation and feeling of inferiority among them.

   C. It is a matter of grave concern that "stress" or "mental pressure" has emerged as a deadly and silent killer for teenagers of the day.

   D. In order to prevent these catastrophic diseases, children need to be taught to de-stress themselves through meditation or cultural activities and this will inculcate feelings of self-confidence in them and inspire them to face the realities of life in a better way.

   E. If they are observed closely, this all owes to undue pressure on their mind due to unhealthy competitions and sky rocketing expectations of their parents and teachers from them.

Your answer: _____

TASK TWO
Using Transition Words and Phrases Properly

ACTIVITY ▶

Learning to use transitions properly in writing

Step 1

Read the following paragraphs and underline transition words and phrases used in the paragraphs.

Paragraph 1

I do well in school, and people think I am smart because of it. But it's not true. In fact, three years ago I struggled in school. However, two years ago I decided to get serious about school and made a few changes. First, I decided I would become interested in whatever was being taught, regardless of what other people thought. I also decided I would work hard every day and never give up on any assignment. I decided to never, never fall behind. Finally, I decided to make school a priority over friends and fun. After implementing these changes, I became an active participant in classroom discussions. Then my test scores began to rise. I still remember the first time that someone made fun of me because "I was smart." How exciting! It seems to me that being smart is simply a matter of working hard and being interested. After all, learning a new video game is a hard work even when you are interested. Unfortunately, learning a new video game doesn't help you get into college or get a good job.

Paragraph 2

The school fair is right around the corner, and tickets have just gone on sale. We are selling a limited number of tickets at a discount, so move fast and get yours while they are still available. This is going to be an event you will not want to miss! First of all, the school fair is a great value when compared with other forms of entertainment. Also, your ticket purchase will help our school, and when you help the school, it helps the entire community. But that's not all! Every ticket you purchase enters you in a drawing to win fabulous prizes. And don't forget, you will have mountains of fun because there are acres and acres of great rides, fun games, and entertaining attractions! Spend time with your family and friends at our school fair. Buy your tickets now!

Paragraph 3

People often install a kitty door, only to discover that they have a problem. The problem is that their cat will not use the kitty door. There are several common reasons why cats won't use kitty doors. First, they may not understand how a kitty door works. They may not understand that it is a little doorway just for them. Second, many kitty doors are dark and cats cannot see to the other side. As a result, they can't be sure of what is on the other side of the door, so they won't take the risk. One last reason cats won't use kitty doors is because some cats don't like the feeling of pushing through and then having the door drag across their back. But don't worry—there are solutions to this problem.

Step 2

Discuss in groups and answer the following questions.

1. Why are transition words and phrases used? What will the paragraphs be like if there is no transition word or phrase used?
2. What kinds of meanings are expressed by different transition words and phrases in these paragraphs?
3. What other kinds of transition words or phrases do you know? Give examples.

Step 3

Work in groups and classify transition words and phrases according to their different uses，meanings and forms．

Types of Transitions	Transition Words	Transition Phrases
to add more information	besides，furthermore，…	In addition，…
to indicate an example		
to indicate cause or reason		
to indicate result or effect		
to indicate purpose		
to compare or contrast		
to explain time sequence		
to make concession		
to emphasize		
to summarize		
to conclude		

Module 15　Achieving Coherence in Paragraph Writing

Read the following paragraphs and fill in blanks with proper transition words or phrases to make the paragraphs coherent.

1. In the last twenty years or so, some undeveloped countries have increased their food production. Their population, (1) _____, have at the same time grown faster. And (2) _____ their standard of living has not been improved. (3) _____, their increase in food production has been achieved at the expense of using up marginal lands. (4) _____, there has been no gain in the productivity of land labor.

2. The ancient Egyptians were masters of preserving dead people's bodies by making mummies of them. (1) _____, mummification consisted of removing the internal organs, applying natural preservatives inside and out, and then wrapping the body in layers of bandages. (2) _____ the process was remarkably effective. (3) _____, mummies of several thousand years old have been discovered nearly intact. Their skin, hair, teeth, fingernails and toenails, and facial features are still evident. Their diseases in life, (4) _____ smallpox, arthritis, and nutritional deficiencies, are still diagnosable. (5) _____ their fatal afflictions are (6) _____ apparent: a middle-aged king died from a blow on the head; a child king died from polio.

3. Vegetables and fruits are an important part of a healthy diet. (1) _____, fruits and vegetables are packed with the vitamins and minerals you need to keep your body functioning smoothly. (2) _____, they give you the carbohydrates you need for energy. Fruits and vegetables have lots of fiber to help your digestive system work properly. (3) _____, many scientists believe that the nutrients in fruits and vegetables can help fight diseases. (4) _____, if you eat a diet rich in fruits and vegetables, you'll be on the road to a better health.

TASK THREE
Using Pronouns to Avoid Repetition

ACTIVITY ▶

Learning to use pronouns properly

Step 1

Read the following two paragraphs and underline the parts where there are differences.

Paragraph 1

Don't be misled by the British tendency to be soft-spoken and polite. If they need to they can be plenty tough. The English language didn't spread across the oceans and over the mountains and jungles and swamps of the world because these people were panty-waists.

Paragraph 2

Don't be misled by the British tendency to be soft-spoken and polite. If the British need to the British can be plenty tough. The English language didn't spread across the oceans and over the mountains and jungles and swamps of the world because the British were panty-waists.

Step 2

Work in pairs and discuss which paragraph above is better in its wording.

Step 3

Work in pairs and improve the following paragraph, based on your discussion in Step 2.

Mr. Thompson agreed to meet with members of the worker's union before Mr. Thompson signed the contract. Mr. Thompson was interested in hearing the union members' concerns about the new insurance plan.

Your improvement

TASK FOUR
Using Necessary Repetitions in Writing

ACTIVITY ▶

Learning to use repetitions properly

Step 1

Read the following paragraphs. Pay close attention to the underlined parts.

Paragraph 1

For a politician <u>power</u> is the name of the game. The <u>power</u> to be heard, the <u>power</u> to decide and, ultimately, the <u>power</u> to shape events. Without <u>power</u>, what use are policies? A politician without <u>power</u> is like a yachtsman with no wind-becalmed, bemused, going nowhere.

Paragraph 2

<u>There are couples who dislike one another</u> furiously for several hours at a time; <u>there are couples who dislike one another</u> permanently; and <u>there are couples who</u> never dislike one another; but these last are people who are incapable of disliking anybody.

Paragraph 3

At the museum, the class <u>attended a lecture where the speaker demonstrated</u> how the Native Americans made bows and arrows. They also <u>attended a lecture where a sword smith demonstrated</u> how the Vikings crafted swords.

Step 2

Work in groups of 3-4 members and have a discussion on the following questions.

The underlined parts in the three paragraphs above are regarded as necessary repetition. Discuss the questions to understand how coherence are achieved through repetition:

1. What effects do the repetitions have on the writing of each paragraph?
2. Do you think the repetitions in the three paragraphs are of the same type? Why?
3. What items can be repeated according to the examples in these paragraphs?

> **To achieve coherence in paragraph writing, we can:**
> - arrange sentences in proper order;
> - use transition words and phrases;
> - use pronouns to avoid repetition;
> - use necessary repetitions properly.

ASSIGNMENTS

1. Re-arrange the order of the following sentences to construct a coherent paragraph.

A. Then, with a popular film, I usually have to wait in a long line at the ticket booth.

B. Although I love movies, going to see them drives me slightly crazy.

C. All in all, I would rather stay home and wait for the latest movie hits to appear on TV in the safety and comfort of my own living room.

D. First of all, getting to the movie can take a lot of time. I have a thirty five-minute drive down a congested highway.

E. Another problem is that the theater itself is seldom a pleasant place to be.

F. Kids run up and down the aisle. Teenagers laugh and shout at the screen.

G. Half the seats seem to be falling apart. And the floor often has a sticky coating that gets on your shoes.

H. People of all ages loudly drop soda cups and popcorn tubs, cough and burp, and elbow you out of the armrest on either side of your seat.

I. A musty smell suggests that there has been no fresh air in the theater since it was built.

J. The worst problem of all is some of the other moviegoers.

Your answer: _____

2. **Read the following paragraphs and fill in blanks with proper transition words or phrases to make the paragraphs coherent.**

A. One day, I saw a homeless man who was a little bit different from other homeless people. When he got onto the bus, he started making a speech: how hard he had tried to find a job, how difficult it was to do so, how hungry he was, and so on. (1) _____ he sang a song with a sad low voice. It sounded pitiful throughout the bus. (2) _____, his speech was so persuasive that people could not help feeling sympathy. (3) _____, most people there gave him some change, or even a dollar. His paper cup was filled with money in a minute.

B. During my father's generation, the education system was very different. Back in those days, most schools were provided by the British. In those days, people had a better education than nowadays (1) _____ teachers had different ways of teaching. Most of the students were taught by British native teachers. (2) _____, they spoke better English and had high standards in English. Also, they began learning English in primary school. (3) _____, all of the subjects were taught in English. The schools' rules were strictly followed, and they had punishments for every little thing. In my generation, the educational system was far different from my father's. (4) _____, all the subjects were taught in Burmese except for English. I myself and other students from my generation started to learn English in the fifth grade. In each grade, we must pass every subject. (5) _____, we must repeat that particular grade. (6) _____, it was really hard to graduate from high school. (7) _____ tenth grade, we can enter college. In the old days, there was no limit in choosing any major or professional field that we wanted. Things were not easy in my generation. The students had fewer opportunities to learn.

3. Read the paragraph below and figure out the ways used to make the paragraph coherent.

Throughout most of my school days my eyes failed to focus correctly when reading. Consequently, I saw different symbols every time I read a sentence. As a result, the printed page was a chaotic kaleidoscope of constantly changing letters that made no sense. For example, when reading the last sentence I would see: "Atters made sense," or "As le ter that made no ense," or "Letters mad no sens," depending on how my eyes focused on a sentence. After my eye problem was corrected, my real problems began because it was assumed that I could now read like everyone else. This was a big mistake that overlooked the psychological effects created by my visual disability. Most importantly, I was left doubting my understanding when reading unfamiliar material while teachers began to give me increasingly complex material to read.

Module 16   Achieving Completeness in Paragraph Writing

When finishing the learning of this module,

Goal 1   I will know locations of topic sentences in a paragraphs.

Goal 2   I will know how to support a topic sentence with proper developing sentences.

Goal 3   I will know how to conclude a paragraph.

Goal 4   I will understand ways of development in paragraph writing.

Section 2   Writing a Good Paragraph (1) • • • • • • • • • •

TASK ONE
Achieving Completeness in Paragraph Writing

ACTIVITY 1 ▶

Identifying the topic sentence in a paragraph

Step 1

Work in pairs and find out or generalize the topic sentence of each paragraph. If there is an obvious topic sentence (TS), highlight the topic and underline the controlling idea. If you don't think there is a TS in a paragraph, generalize its main idea in a sentence.

1. The park is a pleasant place for everyone. Little kids like to play on the swings and slides. Older children can play little league baseball or other team sports at the larger parks. Teenagers often play Frisbee on the grass or volleyball in

the sand. Adults enjoy taking walks, and some seniors like to sit on the park benches and feed the birds.

- **Topic sentence/Main idea:**

2. Some people leave too many lights on around the house. Some aren't careful about how much water they use. Americans waste a lot of resources. Most people buy products with a lot of unnecessary packagings that aren't good for the environment.

- **Topic sentence/Main idea:**

3. The Amazon River is the widest river in the world, with one-fifth of all the fresh water on earth moving through its mouth. In length it is the second only to the Nile, and if stretched across the United States, it would reach from New York to Los Angeles. In addition, the Amazon covers the largest area of any river. Therefore, it can't be argued that the Amazon is the mightiest river on earth.

- **Topic sentence/Main idea:**

4. Dogs in the U.S. are treated like humans. People talk to their dogs and buy them special toys and clothings. There are special parks, hotels, restaurants, and bakeries for dogs. Some owners take their dogs to see psychiatrist as well as the veterinarian. American dogs are spoiled like kids.

- **Topic sentence/Main idea:**

5. I'm over 21 years of age. I'm a citizen of the United States. I have not been convicted of a felony. And I have not been treated or confined for drug addiction, drunkenness, or mental illness. According to the National Firearms of Act of 1934, I thus qualify for purchasing a fully automatic machine gun which is capable of firing hundreds of bullets with a single squeeze of the trigger.

- **Topic sentence/Main idea:**

Module 16　Achieving Completeness in Paragraph Writing

Step 2

Work together with another pair and answer the following questions.

1. Where is the topic sentence found in each paragraph?
2. Where do you think is the best place for a topic sentence? Why?
3. What effect can different locations of topic sentence have on a paragraph?
4. If there is no obvious topic sentence, how do we figure out the main idea of that paragraph?

Step 3

Discuss and summarize the intentional effects of different locations of a topic sentence (TS).

1. TS at the beginning: to state the topic and controlling idea directly _____
2. TS in the middle of a paragraph: _____
3. TS at the end of a paragraph: _____
4. TS at the beginning and at the end: _____
5. TS understated (implied): _____

ACTIVITY 2 ▶

Understanding developing sentences for full development

Step 1

Read the following three paragraphs and then answer questions after your reading.

Paragraph 1

　　Taking part in sports can also help improve study efficiency. It can give you a rest after a day's hard work. It can make you relax when you feel tired and broken-down. It can relieve the pressure you have in studies. If you take part in sports regularly, your study efficiency will surely be improved.

Paragraph 2

<u>Taking part in sports can also help improve study efficiency.</u> One study shows that people who take regular exercise suffer less from anxiety and are able to work harder. According to a medical report，83 percent of the freshmen who had trouble with studies were in bad physical shape. And when they were put into a physical fitness program，their grades were picked up more or less.

Paragraph 3

<u>Taking part in sports can also help improve study efficiency.</u> For example，whenever I feel a little tired from studies，I will have a 15-minute walk on campus. After a brief walk I always feel entirely refreshed and relaxed. I can continue to study and memorize things better. My personal experience shows that half an hour's exercise after supper will help you maintain concentration for a whole night.

Questions

1. Are the paragraphs unified，coherent and complete?
2. Do all the developing sentences focus on and support the topic sentence?
3. How do the developing sentences in each paragraph support the topic sentence? Are they major developing sentences or minor developing sentences?
4. Is there any difference in the supporting evidence provided in each paragraph?
5. Which paragraph do you think explain the idea more adequately? Why?
6. How do you think should developing sentences be used to support a topic sentence?

Developing Sentences
1. **Providing adequate supporting ideas and details for full development**
   - **Major developing sentences** provide general supporting ideas.
   - **Minor developing sentences** provide specific supporting details，like examples，facts，statistics，reasons，stories，personal experiences，etc.
2. **Having effective organization of supporting ideas**
   - with clear sections of different ideas and details
   - being arranged in logical，chronological or spatial order，or in the order of importance，etc.

Module 16　Achieving Completeness in Paragraph Writing

Find out problems in the following paragraphs and make proper improvements.

1. There are three reasons why John is not going to university. In the first place, his family is quite poor, and since he has four young brothers and sisters still at school, he feels he should help his family financially as soon as possible. Secondly, if he went to university, his mother would be left alone to look after the young children. Consequently, although he wants to go to university very much, John is going to take the job instead.

   - **Your improved paragraph:**

2. Here is the perfect system for cleaning your room. First, move all of the items that do not have a proper place to the center of the room. Get rid of at least five things that you have not used within the last year. Take out all of the trash, and place all of the dirty dishes in the kitchen sink. See, that was easy!

   - **Your improved paragraph:**

Step 3

Write proper developing sentences to support the following topic sentences.

1. I like listening to music because it helps me to relax.

2. There are several advantages of online shopping.

Step 4

Work in pairs and evaluate your partner's work in Step 3 with the checklist below.

Checklist

☐ There is a topic sentence stating the topic and the controlling idea of the paragraph.

☐ There are major developing sentences expressing supporting ideas, and minor developing sentences providing supporting details.

☐ There are enough supporting ideas and specific details (examples, statistics, facts, etc.) provided to fully develop the paragraph.

☐ All the supporting ideas and details are closely related to and support the main idea.

☐ The developing sentences can be divided into different sections, according to the ideas they express.

☐ All the sentences are arranged in an appropriate order.

☐ There is proper use of transition words or phrases.

Step 5

Discuss your evaluations with your partner.

ACTIVITY 3 ▶

Understanding the different ways to conclude a paragraph

Module 16 Achieving Completeness in Paragraph Writing

Read the following paragraphs and identify different ways of concluding a paragraph.

1. Here is the perfect system for cleaning your room. First, move all of the items that do not have a proper place to the center of the room. Get rid of at least five things that you have not used within the last year. Take out all of the trash, and place all of the dirty dishes in the kitchen sink. Now find a location for each of the items you had placed in the center of the room. For any remaining items, see if you can squeeze them in under your bed or stuff them into the back of your closet. See, that was easy!
   - **Way of concluding:**

2. Last year was the first time I had ever been the new kid at school. For the first four days, I was completely alone. I don't think I even spoke to a single person. Finally, at lunch on the fifth day, Karen Watson walked past her usual table and sat down right next to me. Even though I was new, I had already figured out who Karen Watson was. She was popular. Pretty soon, all of Karen's friends were sitting there right next to me. I never became great friends with Karen, but after lunch that day, it seemed like all sorts of people were happy to be my friend. You cannot convince me that Karen did not know what she was doing. I have a great respect for her, and I learned a great deal about what it meant to be a true leader.
   - **Way of concluding:**

3. People often install a kitty door, only to discover that they have a problem. The problem is their cat will not use the kitty door. There are several common reasons why cats won't use kitty doors. First, they may not understand how a kitty door works. They may not understand that it is a little doorway just for them. Second, many kitty doors are dark and cats cannot see to the other side. As such, they can't be sure of what is on the other side of the door, so they won't take the risk. One last reason cats won't use kitty doors is because

some cats don't like the feeling of pushing through and then having the door drag across their back. But don't worry—there are solutions to this problem.

• **Way of concluding**:

Step 2

Discuss in groups of 3-4 members and answer the following questions.

1. How is each paragraph closed? What kind of idea is expressed in each concluding sentence?
2. What is the use of a concluding sentence in paragraph writing?
3. Are there other ways to close a paragraph? What are they? Give some examples.

TASK TWO

Understanding Ways of Development in Paragraph Writing

ACTIVITY ▶

Analyzing and identifying the ways of development

Step 1

Read the information box below.

Ways of Development/Ways to Develop a Paragraph

1. **From general to specific**

   With topic sentence at the beginning, followed by developing sentences

2. **From specific to general**

   Opening from developing sentences, with topic sentence given at the end

Module 16 Achieving Completeness in Paragraph Writing

Reread the following paragraphs from TASK ONE, underline the topic sentence, and figure out the way of development in each paragraph.

1. The park is a pleasant place for everyone. Little kids like to play on the swings and slides. Older children can play little league baseball or other team sports at the larger parks. Teenagers often play Frisbee on the grass or volleyball in the sand. Adults enjoy taking walks, and some seniors like to sit on the park benches and feed the birds.
   • **Way of development:**

2. The Amazon River is the widest river in the world, with one-fifth of all the fresh water on earth moving through its mouth. In length it is second only to the Nile, and if stretched across the United States, it would reach from New York to Los Angeles. In addition, the Amazon covers the largest area of any river. Therefore, it can't be argued that the Amazon is the mightiest river on earth.
   • **Way of development:**

3. Dogs in the U.S. are treated like humans. People talk to their dogs and buy them special toys and clothings. There are special parks, hotels, restaurants, and bakeries for dogs. Some owners take their dogs to see psychiatrist as well as the veterinarian. American dogs are spoiled like kids.
   • **Way of development:**

Step 3

Work in groups of 3-4 members and discuss why different ways of development are used.

ASSIGNMENTS

Write paragraphs on the same topic "public bike-sharing (单车共享) in China",
using more than two different ways of development introduced in Step 1,
TASK TWO.

1. There are many advantages of public bike-sharing. _____

_____

_____

_____

_____

_____

2. _____

_____

_____

_____

_____

Obviously, there are also problems in public bike-sharing.

3. Now that shared bikes are a convenient way for users to get around, users
should follow the rules to make sure that shared bikes will bring greater
advantages to more people. _____

_____

_____

_____

_____

Only in this way can public bike-sharing be beneficial to people and to our
environment.

List of Sources

本书在编写时，为了保证语言纯正地道，我们参考了部分来源于国内外网站的语句和文章段落，在此罗列清单，并对原作者表示感谢。

http://advice.writing.utoronto.ca/revising/passive-voice/

http://blog.lessonenglishgrammar.com/2014/10/paragraph-rearrangement-of-sentences-to.html

http://cn.bing.com/images/search? q＝bad＋paragraph＋examples&qpvt＝bad＋paragraph＋examples&FORM＝IGRE

http://grammar.ccc.commnet.edu/grammar/paragraphs.htm

http://grammar.ccc.commnet.edu/GRAMMAR/quizzes/runons_quiz.htm

http://grammar.ccc.commnet.edu/Grammar/transitions.htm

http://kedatgym204.wikispaces.com/file/view/exercises_on_paragraph_writing.pdf

http://patternbasedwriting.com/elementary_writing_success/paragraph-examples/

http://slulibrary.saintleo.edu/c.php? g＝367733&p＝2485890

http://write-site.athabascau.ca/documentation/Sample％20of％20a％20coherent％20paragraph.pdf

http://www.docin.com/p-1024210413.html

http://www.preservearticles.com/201107149072/list-of-six-sample-paragraphs-for-middle-school-students.html

http://www.southeastern.edu/acad_research/programs/writing_center/handouts/pdf_handouts/coherence.pdf

http://www.syracusecityschools.com/tfiles/folder836/Research％20TRANSITION％20WORDS％20AND％20PHRASES.pdf

http://www.tceic.com/ig1l8h6lh84gk45i3h358i0j.html

http://www.tceic.com/kg9k83g2680203j8ik2l24g1.html

http://www.wendangku.net/doc/00d7111876eeaeaad1f330f3.html

http://www.wwnorton.com/college/english/write/we/ch5/17c.htm

https://boingboing.net/2012/11/13/instructions-for-american-serv.html

https://k12.thoughtfullearning.com/studentmodels/friendship

https://members.123helpme.com/document/18946

https://owl.purdue.edu/owl/general_writing/mechanics/sentence_fragments.html

https：//patternbasedwriting. com/elementary_writing_success/paragraph-examples/

https：//sites. google. com/site/boostgrammarbank/collocations-about-vs-of/common-collocation-errors

https：//sun. iwu. edu/～writcent/shifts&mixed_construction. html

https：//webapps. towson. edu/ows/faultycomp. htm

https：//webapps. towson. edu/ows/moduleDangling. htm

https：//webapps. towson. edu/ows/modulepro. htm

https：//wenku. baidu. com/view/07c66b40bd64783e09122bc8. html

https：//wenku. baidu. com/view/365392ed856a561252d36f7d. html

https：//wenku. baidu. com/view/5293ba038e9951e79a892750. html

https：//wenku. baidu. com/view/7af88fd49b89680203d82590. html

https：//wenku. baidu. com/view/9458a25bf524ccbff021843b. html? from＝search

https：//wenku. baidu. com/view/f33d383c0b4c2e3f57276329. html? sxts＝1532851614939

https：//writingcenter. unc. edu/tips-and-tools/paragraphs/

https：//www. csun. edu/sites/default/files/Auerbach-Handout-Paragraph-Writing-Examples. pdf

https：//www. ecenglish. com/learnenglish/lessons/how-use-reported-speech

https：//www. ef. com/english-resources/english-grammar/singular-and-plural-nouns/

https：//www. e-grammar. org/reported-speech/

https：//www. eurocentres. com/blog/direct-and-indirect-speech-whats-the-difference/

https：//www. gingersoftware. com/content/grammar-rules/verbs/modal-verbs/

https：//www. grammarbank. com/irrelevant-sentences-paragraph. html

https：//www. learnamericanenglishonline. com/Orange％ 20Level/O5％ 20Compound-Complex％
20Sentences. html

https：//www. learnenglish. de/grammar/reportedspeech. html

https：//www. swarthmore. edu/writing/mixed-constructions-0

https：//www. thoughtco. com/collocation-examples-1210325

https：//www. thoughtco. com/compound-complex-sentence-grammar-1689870

https：//www. thoughtco. com/inversion-definition-1209968

https：//www. thoughtco. com/model-descriptive-paragraphs-1690573

https：//www. thoughtco. com/repeating-key-words-and-structures-1690555

https：//www. uhv. edu/student-success-center/resources/e-p/faulty-comparison/

https：//www. writing. com/main/view_item/item_id/927399-How-To-Write-A-Good-Paragraph